S0-BXC-619

What's on

The CD-ROM accompanying *YOUR MONEY* includes many of the useful financial worksheets and programs discussed in the book, plus $15 worth of free time on CompuServe, the most popular and comprehensive online service in the country.

For starters, you'll find a wide variety of useful spreadsheets in three common formats—Lotus 1-2-3, Microsoft Works, and Microsoft Excel—to help you

- Manage your checkbook and credit card payments
- Create inventories of your household contents for insurance
- Compare types of insurance to see which one is best for you
- Track home and car purchase costs
- Project the cost of tuition and estimate how much you'll need to save each year
- Determine how much money you'll need to save for retirement

In addition, you'll find several programs designed to make financial planning easier for you and your family. These programs will help you to

- Track the value of your savings bonds
- Compare fixed-rate and adjustable-rate mortgages
- Compare the costs of buying points on a mortgage and buying a mortgage with no points

You'll also find on this CD a copy of WinCIM software for Windows, your pathway to the online world.

Look inside... and start your financial planning today. You can't afford to wait!

System Requirements

- 386DX-33 (486DX-33 or faster recommended)
- 4MB RAM (minimum)

- 4MB available on hard drive
- SuperVGA adapter (supporting 640 X 480 resolution and 256 colors) highly recommended
- Microsoft mouse or 100% compatible
- Microsoft Windows 3.1 or higher
- MS-DOS 3.0 or higher
- Single-speed CD-ROM drive (double-speed recommended)

See Appendix A for instructions on using the CD-ROM that accompanies this book.

YOUR MONEY:
Total **Financial**
Planning on
Your **Computer**

YOUR MONEY:
Total Financial Planning on Your Computer

Gus Venditto

ZIFF-DAVIS PRESS
EMERYVILLE, CALIFORNIA

Development Editor	Mary Johnson
Copy Editors	Mary Johnson and Kelly Green
Project Coordinator	Ami Knox
Cover Illustration	Regan Honda
Cover Design	Regan Honda
Cover Copy	Sean Kelly
Book Design	Regan Honda
Technical Illustration	Sarah Isida, Cherie Plumlee
Word Processing	Howard Blechman
Page Layout	M.D. Barrera
Indexer	Valerie Robbins

Ziff-Davis Press books are produced on a Macintosh computer system with the following applications: FrameMaker®, Microsoft® Word, QuarkXPress®, Adobe Illustrator®, Adobe Photoshop®, Adobe Streamline™, MacLink®*Plus*, Aldus® FreeHand™, Collage Plus™.

If you have comments or questions or would like to receive a free catalog, call or write:
Ziff-Davis Press
5903 Christie Avenue
Emeryville, CA 94608
1-800-688-0448

To Ann, Joe, and Michael, for the knowledge and the values.

Table of Contents

viii **Starting Out**

Chapter 1   *Getting Organized*   **1**
- **2**   Clearing the Clutter
- **5**   The Papers You'll Need
- **7**   Choosing Your Tools
- **14**   Build Security into Your Plan

Chapter 2   *Assembling a Household Budget*   **17**
- **19**   Setting Up Your Accounts
- **24**   Recording Your First Transactions
- **28**   Fine-Tuning Your Accounts
- **30**   Managing Quicken Data Files
- **30**   Building a Spreadsheet Check Register
- **33**   Ready for the Future

Chapter 3   *Trimming the Fat*   **37**
- **40**   Let Quicken Do Your Budget
- **42**   Adjusting Categories to Reflect Spending
- **44**   Tracking Your Cash
- **46**   Making Credit Cards Work for You
- **50**   Shopping for Value Online

Chapter 4   *Investing Wisely: Mutual Funds*   **55**
- **56**   Mutual Fund Basics
- **61**   Choosing a Fund Strategy
- **63**   Shopping for Mutual Funds Online
- **70**   Keeping Track of Your Funds

Chapter 5   *Investing: Stocks*   **75**
- **76**   What Online Services Can—and Can't—Do
- **78**   How to Research Stocks with Dow Jones
- **80**   Researching Stocks with CompuServe
- **85**   How to Research Stocks with Prodigy
- **88**   How to Research Stocks on the Internet
- **90**   Trading with Online Brokers

Chapter 6   *Saving at the Highest Rates*   **95**
- **96**   Finding the Best Savings Bank Interest Rates
- **98**   Calculating the Value of Savings Bonds

Chapter 7   *Protecting Your Kingdom*   **105**

106   Assessing Your Life Insurance Needs
110   Shopping for a Life Insurance Policy
116   Creating a Home Inventory

Chapter 8   *Shopping for Loans and Mortgages*   **125**

127   The New Car Decision: A Spreadsheet Can Help
135   Buying a House: Figuring What You Can Afford
138   Shopping for Mortgages

Chapter 9   *Paying for College*   **145**

146   Shopping for Colleges
149   Creating a Strategy for Your College Fund
154   A Monthly Savings Plan: How Much Is Enough?

Chapter 10   *Saving Time and Money on Your Taxes*   **159**

160   How to Get Ahead of the Tax Game
164   How to Get Quicken to Track Tax Expenses
168   Working Smarter in TurboTax

Chapter 11   *Planning for Retirement*   **175**

176   How Much Income Will You Need?
181   Projecting the Growth of Your Savings
185   How Long Will Your Savings Last?
188   Getting the Most from Your Savings

Chapter 12   *Estate Planning*   **191**

192   Why You Need a Will
195   What You Can and Can't Do with WillMaker
199   Creating a Living Will
201   Organize Your Records for Posterity

Appendix A   *Guide to the CD-ROM*   **204**

Appendix B   *Where to Find It*   **207**

209   *Index*

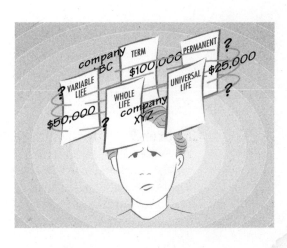

Financial planning isn't hard. You've been doing it all your life.

Starting out as an infant, you knew how to get what you needed with a plaintive cry. As you learned more and your needs became more refined, you devised elaborate plans to get the necessities of life, like trendy clothes and gas money.

By the time you were on your own, you had a very simple plan: to make it to the next paycheck. Few of us make it past this instinctive style of planning. With food on the table and credit cards at hand, financial planning sounds like a luxury. It's something that the rich do in oak-paneled rooms, over cigars and brandy.

Not anymore. Not in the '90s with an economy that bounds from one uncertainty to another. Not in a country that doesn't know what it will do when the Social Security fund runs dry.

Financial planning has become a necessity. Everyone needs to create a safety net to protect against unexpected problems. And unless you're working for one of the last companies in America offering a full pension, you need to build and manage your own retirement fund.

Now for the good news; financial planning is not expensive. It is not time-consuming. And it's not hard work, especially with a personal computer available to work the numbers.

For most people, creating a financial plan and sticking to it will use up only a few more minutes a week, time that is now probably eaten up solving one minor financial crisis or another.

Creating a financial plan will give you more from life. You'll earn more from your savings, and you'll spend less than you would otherwise. Most important, you'll have more control over your life.

A financial plan is not a miracle cure. It won't create vast riches from a handful of dollars. Your financial plan is a means to an end. It's the strategy you'll follow to make sure you can do the things you want. It will force you to set priorities; you'll have to deny yourself some pleasures for the sake of others. And you'll have to do some hard thinking: You need to decide on the goals that are most important for you and your family. If you're ready to make the effort, this book will help you get there. It will guide you through the tools available for a personal computer and help you make the most of both your time and your money.

What You'll Need

- ✔ A PC running Windows
- ✔ A spreadsheet like Microsoft Works, Lotus 1-2-3, or Microsoft Excel
- ✔ A modem to connect to online services
- ✔ A CD-ROM player to run the spreadsheets and software programs on the CD that comes with this book

If you already use Quicken, this book will give you lots of ideas on how to get more from it. If you don't use Quicken already, this book should convince you to give this personal financial program a try.

That's all you'll need. Having a printer will come in handy, and along the way I'll tell you about other programs that may be nice to have, but the goal here is to help you build wealth and get your finances under control without eating up all of your free time and discretionary income.

You'll learn basic techniques for improving your money-management skills, and you'll get some advice on occasion. But nothing too specific. This book is about helping you take control of your own money and learn how to make the decisions that are right for you. Your computer can be a useful tool, but the choices will be yours to make.

And since this book provides you with spreadsheet files along with help in using them, you'll have a set of tools you can use for years to come. As a result, you'll be making better decisions when you borrow money, make major purchases, and plan for your future.

Planning is an ongoing process. I'd love to hear from you on how you've used the ideas in this book. You can reach me on CompuServe at 72241,42 and on Prodigy at BYFJ62A; on the Interchange Online Network, you can simply write to GusVenditto.

1

Getting Organized

2 Clearing the Clutter

5 The Papers You'll Need

7 Choosing Your Tools

14 Build Security into Your Plan

Getting

organized is the best way to boost your efforts to develop a successful system for financial planning. The sooner you get your financial affairs in order, the easier it will be to make sound decisions about your future.

Trying to build your financial future without making records of your expenses is like playing with sand. It's this lack of control that makes it seem like money is slipping through your fingers. In the following chapters we'll look at the many ways that you can gain power over your finances instead of letting them overpower you. But first things first: Create a system for tracking your money and stick with it.

Clearing the Clutter

There's no perfect system for keeping financial records. Salvation does not lie in a particular combination of color-coded folders and index cards. You want a routine that will give you easy access to the records you need and that will save time by getting receipts, bills, statements, and so on out of your hair as soon as possible.

Here's where your computer comes in. You can use it to record the transactions that make up the business of your life. (See the next section, "Choosing Your Tools," for details.) Then, you are free to dispose of the messy paper bills and account statements that can choke your record system. Evaluate each piece of paper by asking yourself "Will I need this?" If not, get rid of it.

You can't eliminate paper completely. Some records can't be duplicated and others, like insurance policies and leases, have very specific information that sets out contractual obligations. So you will need some kind of filing system, but be kind to yourself and make your system easy to maintain. Here are some guidelines that may lighten the load:

- Get a filing cabinet or storage cases that are designed for paper documents.
- Make sure you have a metal cabinet that can withstand a fire or flood.
- Don't waste money on locks unless you're guarding valuable jewels. It's fire and flood you must guard against, not robbery. Thieves will break the lock off a metal cabinet in less time than it took them to get inside

your house or, even worse, they'll grab the box with your records thinking there's something more valuable than canceled checks and life insurance policies. If they can see it, they probably won't want it.

● Keep your records in a handy place because if they are in a part of the house you seldom visit, you'll make filing more of a chore than is necessary.

● Overcome your fear of bureaucracy and buy folders with tabs so you can label each category in your files. Start by labeling the folders with categories that are based around your mail: each bank account, insurance company and mutual fund should get its own folder. File them alphabetically and dump everything into its folder without worrying about chronological order or categories inside the folder.

● Create a system that will be easy for you to maintain. You're not going to be retrieving records often, so don't put more time into filing than it's worth.

● **You can't eliminate paper but you can organize it.**
As you start to get organized, the greatest skill you need to develop is a sense for when to throw papers away. Nothing will slow you down more than wading through piles of papers that are useless.

You're not doing yourself any favors by keeping every bill and statement. You'll waste time whenever you need to find anything, and you're burdening yourself with extra work. It's far better to keep a record of important transactions on your PC and only keep hard copies of documents that contain detailed information, such as insurance policies and benefit descriptions from employers that contain the type of specific detail you may need to refer to some day.

You should also retain receipts for large purchases because they are the only acceptable proof if you are due a refund, repair, or exchange.

> *Evaluate each piece of paper by asking yourself "Will I need this?" If not, get rid of it.*

But many of the bills you receive, especially those for services like cable TV, phone, and electricity, shouldn't be kept unless you run a business from home and need these bills for a home-office deduction. And while throwing away official looking documents from a bank seems reckless, the fact is, unless you're holding a passbook savings account, most bank statements need to be kept only until you've checked them for accuracy.

A good policy is to review checking and savings account statements for possible errors when they arrive, and then to discard the old statement. Examine the statement to make sure the bank has not tacked on charges that you dispute, and reconcile the checking account with your own register. You always want a recent copy of these account records so you can contact the bank in case you need to close your account or make a change to it, but once you're satisfied the account record is up-to-date, you don't need the old statement. Records for CDs (certificates of deposits) and other fixed-length savings accounts should be held until the end of the term. Savings passbooks should be discarded when the account is closed.

The deed to your home belongs in a safe-deposit box, along with any other records that could help document the value of your possessions in case of fire. Your homeowner's policy can stay with the rest of your records in the house but you should keep a list of insurance policies and agents in the safe-deposit box.

As you're getting organized, don't put all of your emphasis on money. This is also a good time to create folders for other vital categories like medical records. Once you've created a folder for medical records, it will be easy to build your own medical history; just file the receipts your doctor gives you for insurance claims and keep the notices that your insurance company sends after you submit a claim.

Is It Worth Keeping?

✔ Does it support your tax return?

✔ Will it serve as a proof of purchase?

✔ Is it part of your financial history?

The Papers You'll Need

There are only three reasons you need to keep records:

➡ Conforming with the tax code

➡ Supplying a proof of purchase

➡ Your own financial planning

The tax laws give the Internal Revenue Service up to three years to audit your return, and an additional three years to audit only if there's suspicion that income was underreported by more than 25 percent. So any records that support your position in a fight with the IRS should be kept for six years. The most obvious papers you'll need are receipts that prove deductions, but if you've got an unusual situation, you may want to keep more than that. For example, if you claimed a deduction for the expense of moving to a new job and the job didn't work out, you will want to keep a letter that proves you were offered the job.

Proof of purchase serves two purposes. It can ensure that you get your money's worth on a purchase, and it can validate ownership of an item if you need to claim a loss. You should keep a receipt as long as you think it will help you get a refund or exchange if the merchandise proves defective. For instance, expensive stereo equipment usually comes with a warranty, and if the sound dies before the warranty is up, most stores will want to see your receipt, even two years later.

Receipts will also help you file an insurance claim, especially if you have expensive tastes. For example, if a fire destroys your wardrobe, the insurance company will want to apply average prices to the clothes. If you have a weakness for $900 silk suits, protect that habit by saving your receipts. Sometimes you can use credit card statements to help support a claim, but they're less reliable than the actual receipt.

Finally, you need to keep records to do your own financial planning. They'll be indispensible when you're ready to create a budget using the credit card statements and utility bills that show where your money is actually going. Fortunately, once you've accurately recorded them in a computer file, you won't need them anymore. After that chore is done, you'll be able to print very detailed transaction lists that identify your income and your outflow.

However, don't throw away all of your old paper records just yet. As you start to create your financial plan, you'll want to create a budget and you'll need many of the bills that will end up being trashed after the details are stored in the computer. You should also hold onto canceled checks. They will serve as your proof of payment if one of your creditors makes an error.

You should use your bank statement to record all transactions and be sure to reconcile them against your check register. You should also use your computer to record all of the transactions on savings and investment account statements before discarding them. Simply make sure you always keep some record for each financial organization where you hold an account so that you can get in touch with them if you want to make a deposit or withdrawal.

An easy record-keeping system is to set aside bank statements, investment statements and credit card bills near your computer. Use your financial software to record each transaction and then, after you've saved the file and made two backup copies on floppy disks, throw away statements you don't need. Store your canceled checks in a metal storage cabinet along with one of the floppy disks. Place the other floppy in a separate location as a safeguard. If you've been keeping old checks, throw away the ones that are more than six years old whenever you add recent ones.

Transactions Your PC Can Track

✔ Check payments

✔ Income

✔ Credit card transactions

✔ Investment purchases
✔ Investment earnings
✔ Bank interest earnings
✔ Loans

Papers Worth Keeping

✔ Canceled checks
✔ Employment contracts
✔ Employee benefit notices
✔ Deeds to property
✔ Insurance policies
✔ Tax returns
✔ Receipts that support tax deductions

NOTE You only need to keep the following kinds of records for a period of six years: canceled checks, tax returns, and receipts that are related to tax deductions. You should get into the habit of routinely discarding all others after recording them in your computer.

Choosing Your Tools

There are two ways to record your financial history on your computer: you can do it by yourself or you can accept some help from experts. The do-it-yourselfer will set everything up on a spreadsheet. The spreadsheet does the math but it's up to you to create categories and to be clever enough to think of all the ways the data can be used.

A better way is to use a personal finance program that will guide you through the process of recording all of your financial information. These programs are designed to make it easy for you to record the important details, and they come with tools that help you use this data for planning.

The basic personal finance toolkit

Using the right tools—a financial program, spreadsheet, online service, and communications software—you're all set to repair your recordkeeping habits.

Quicken from Intuit is the best personal finance program. It does everything other financial programs do and it has two big advantages: It's the easiest to use as well as being the most popular software of its kind. Think of the work you put into entering your Quicken records as an investment in the future; you'll be creating a financial history that can serve you for many years to come. That's not a bad return from a product that costs less than $50.

In the years ahead, banks and credit card companies will be expanding software programs currently in their infancy that will provide access to your accounts through your computer and a modem. Banks will let you transfer money between accounts, pay bills using their software, and transfer account balances from the bank's computer to your own. Credit card companies will let you transfer a copy of your statement from their computer to yours or send you a copy of your monthly statement on a floppy disk. All of these financial records will be accessible to your Quicken registers. One of the reasons Quicken is being recommended throughout this book over competing programs is that it will provide you with more ways to receive financial records in the coming years.

The two closest competitors to Quicken—Managing Your Money and Microsoft Money—do everything that Quicken does. They all are perfectly adequate at recording all of your transactions, calculating your total assets, and helping you plan for the future. If you already own one of these programs, consider switching to Quicken because Quicken is so much friendlier, it actually seems to whisk you through your bookkeeping chores. As you enter one figure, your cursor rests at the next bit of data. You get the job done faster, and with less effort, which means you'll be more likely to keep your financial plan on track.

Quicken whisks you through your chores.

After you enter one letter, Quicken looks up the name from a list.

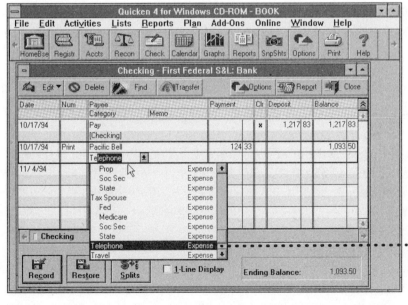

You type in "te" and Quicken finds "telephone" from its list of bill categories.

While Quicken should be the foundation of your financial planning, there are a few other products you can also put to good use. They are discussed in the following sections.

Quicken can help you make many of the financial calculations you'll need, such as retirement planning and loan analysis, but a spreadsheet provides flexibility Quicken lacks. For example, with just a few minutes' work, you can create a spreadsheet that will guide you through the process of buying a car. You can use Quicken to estimate the monthly payment on a loan, but you must build your own spreadsheet if you want details on the specific charges you're faced with. You can shape the spreadsheet to reflect your own way of making the decision, recording the prices you're finding in dealer's showrooms, and then using simple spreadsheet formulas to show you the amounts of your monthly payments. If you can't decide between two option packages, seeing how much they affect your monthly payments may help you decide.

Having trouble deciding between a lease and a loan? No surprise. Leases are notoriously difficult to understand. But you'll be able to determine exactly how much a lease will cost you if you record each lease charge in a spreadsheet and let the spreadsheet do the addition. Most people are shocked at how much extra a car lease costs—if they ever see a real analysis. Most people don't. In Chapter 8, you'll learn how to build a spreadsheet that helps you understand a lease agreement and compare it to a loan.

In addition to Quicken, and a spreadsheet program, the best financial tools you can have are a modem and an account with an online service. Throughout this book you'll learn about money management tips that can only be tapped with one of the online services. From buying stocks to finding the best CD (certificate of deposit) rates available, online services can be invaluable assets that contribute to making you a smarter consumer.

Unfortunately, no online service does it all. CompuServe and Prodigy have the broadest offerings but each has its own unique features. For example, you can shop for the best CD rates on CompuServe, and Prodigy lets you search

Spreadsheets can help you make important decisions.

Any spreadsheet can help you make decisions on big purchases, like a car or mortgage. The examples in this book will use Microsoft Works, but you can use any other spreadsheet just as easily.

	Microsoft Works - [CARBUY.WK1]					
File Edit View Insert Format Tools Window Help						
Arial 12 B I U Σ $						
C22 =PMT((C7+C8-C9),C21/12,C20)						
	A	**B**	**C**	**D**	**E**	**F**
1	**Dealer Cost on Ford Mustang GT**	**$15,534**				
2		**LEASE**	**LOAN**			
3	Target price (MSRP + 7%)	$16,621	$16,621			
4	Options (CD player)	$475	$475			
5	Options (Anti-Lock Braking)	$565	$565			
6	Destination Charge	$475	$475			
7	Price before sales tax	$18,136	$18,136			
8	Sales Tax (6%)	$1,088	$1,088			
9	Down Payment or Capital Cost Red.	$1,000	$3,845			
10						
11	**LEASE CALCULATIONS**					
12	Residual value (50 %)	$10,000				
13	Lease term (months)	36				
14	Lease rate	6.0%				
15	Monthly lease payment	$248				
16	Tax on mo. payment	$15				
17	Total monthly payment	**$262**				
18						
19	**LOAN CALCULATIONS**					
20	Loan term (months)		36			
21	Loan finance rate		8.0%			
22	Monthly payment		**$482**			
23						
Press ALT to choose commands, or F2 to edit.			NUM			

through the full Consumer Reports database. However, each of these features is only available on the respective service.

America Online, Reuters Money Network, and GEnie have enough financial offerings for most people, so if you're a member of any of these services, you may not need to add a second account. But as the range of services on the information highway grows, you're likely to find that you're drawn to more than one online service. So if you've been thinking of opening an account with one service or adding a second, financial planning capabilities may be the extra incentive you need. You'll learn more about the various online services throughout the rest of the book.

NOTE Keep in mind that all of the spreadsheet programs discussed in this book are available in an online service called ZD Press Books Plus. You can access this service from the ZiffNet areas on CompuServe, Prodigy, and Interchange. Among the many tools you'll find on ZD Press Books Plus, there are software utilities that you can use to convert the data from some personal finance programs to a format that Quicken can read.

➔ Tapping the Information Highway

If knowledge is power, then the fastest way to gain power in the '90s is with a modem.

Amazing amounts of information are available through online services that you can tap into using ordinary phone lines with your computer and a modem. If your computer system already has a modem, all you need to do is follow the setup instructions and load the modem's software.

If you still don't own a modem, the decision to take control over your finances is one of the best reasons you'll ever have to take the plunge. When shopping for a modem, you'll find several choices. Here are the factors you need to consider.

➔ **Internal versus external.** An internal modem will be a little more work to set up but it takes up less space, doesn't require a $10 cable, and doesn't use up an electrical outlet. An external modem comes with a display that lets you know when you're online, but if you're not interested in learning more about telecommunications technology, don't bother with it. If you do decide to buy an external modem, before you head to the store, make sure your computer has a serial port (also called a COM port) that's not already taken by another device. If there is no free serial port, you'll need to buy a serial port interface card before you can add an external modem. So you may want to buy an internal modem instead.

Tapping the Information Highway

➡ **2400, 9600 or v.32?** The speed of a modem is identified by its bps (the number of bits it can move in a second). Currently, the most common choice is between 2400 bps, and higher speeds. Don't initially get a 2400 bps modem because the money you save on the price of the modem will be eaten up by the phone connect charges you'll incur. If you want to get the most bang for your buck, choose a V.32 bis or V.FAST modem. Either one will run at 9600 bps or faster, depending on the speed of the service you call.

➡ **Software.** The best choice for a general communications program is ProComm, available either for DOS or Windows. But if you're only planning to call one of the major online services, like CompuServe or Prodigy, you don't need it; you only need software from the service itself. See the Appendix at the back of the book, "Where to Find It," for the phone number for the major online services. If you use CompuServe, try the CIM (CompuServe Information Manager) communications software that is tailored to work with CompuServe, making it easy to find services while you're connected. You can order it directly from CompuServe.

A Serial Port and a Parallel Port

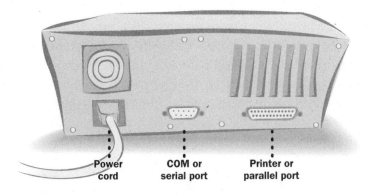

Power cord   COM or serial port   Printer or parallel port

Procomm Plus and a Modem Can Open New Worlds

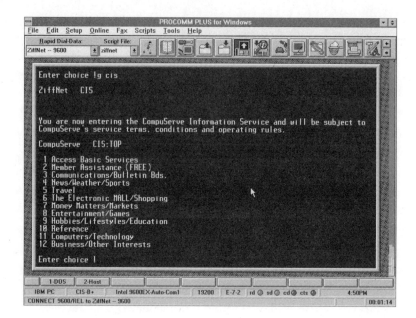

Build Security into Your Plan

Your computer can do many things, but it has one particular talent that is overlooked far too often: It's great at making copies. Any information you enter into the computer can be preserved on a backup copy within seconds and at a cost of mere pennies. Keeping this in mind, don't be shy; make all the backup copies you can stand to have and squirrel them away in secure places. In the unlikely event that your computer is stolen or damaged by fire, the disks stored nearby may be lost as well. A good strategy is to keep an extra disk backup at the desk in your office, and maybe a third disk in the attic for good measure.

As you build your record-keeping system, be sure to remember that backup disks will be a key part of the plan. You don't need to spend money on a backup program; simply copying the files onto a floppy disk is enough. In the following chapters, you'll learn which files are important to back up.

For example, you may want to make a backup copy of the original program disks, such as Quicken and your spreadsheet, but that's not as important as backing up the data you store in your personal disk files. You can always buy another copy of the software if you lose both your hard disk and your floppy disks, but it can be almost impossible to recover large amounts of data that you've recorded over a period of years.

While you're making copies of your financial records, also be sure to create a text file on disk that lists all of your important account information and make a couple of printed copies. A text file is written in a format that any word processor can understand; all word processors have the ability to save files in a text format. You'll want this file in a text format on disk just in case an emergency leaves you without the use of the word processor on your computer and you want to use the file on another PC. Any DOS-compatible PC can read a text file.

Specifically, the text file should contain a list of all bank accounts, insurance companies, mutual fund accounts, stock brokers, and employers—everyone who is holding assets in your name. Record the exact name of the account, account numbers, and the institution's phone number.

Creating a disaster disk isn't the most fun you'll have with your computer, but it may be the best way to buy yourself peace of mind.

2

Assembling a Household Budget

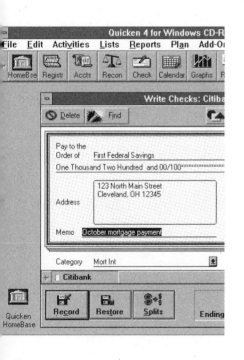

19 Setting Up Your Accounts

24 Recording Your First Transactions

28 Fine-Tuning Your Accounts

30 Managing Quicken Data Files

30 Building a Spreadsheet Check Register

33 Ready for the Future

There's

a time-honored scenario for putting a household on a budget. It usually happens right after a money crisis of some sort. Maybe it's a bounced check that gets your attention, or maybe it's just the realization that you're not saving enough to retire in comfort or to pay for the schools your children are dreaming of attending. So you finally decide to create a household budget and stick with it. You sit down with a pencil and paper (the back of an envelope is good) and you try to add up how much you're spending every month and assign it to a category that will tell you whether the money is necessary or not. Food is important but entertainment can be cut. Chances are, after you've added up everything you can think of—starting with the necessities like the electric bill, gas money, and groceries—you find that there are all kinds of other incidental expenses. The category that seems to eat it all up is "other." Just cut out "other" and you'll have it made! No problem, right? Big problem.

You may feel better after taking a solemn vow to stop spending money on all of your little luxuries like video rentals and eating out. But you won't get anywhere by creating a scapegoat out of these "other" expenses. The biggest portion of your controllable expenses is probably unnecessary but they're also the little pleasures that make you happy. You must live within your means, but if all you do is try to deny yourself favored treats, you'll get nowhere. Like the perennial dieter, in two weeks you'll go on a binge, swearing that there must be a better way.

Adhering to a sensible budget is the only surefire way to turn around a bad financial situation. A budget can serve two crucial purposes: It can be a plan for spending your money the way it will do the most good and it's also a way to make sure you have something left over for savings. The problem with too many budgets is that they're based on rough ideas of what's being spent. The result is that the budget is not based on the real situation.

However, if you start with an accurate summary of what you've been spending in recent months, you'll have a much better chance of gaining control over your money, and making sure you're saving enough to realize your future goals. Your computer can be a big help in performing this task.

The job of recording spending is easy if you enter the amounts of your checks on your computer and assign each payment to a category. You probably will need about 30 minutes a week to tend to all of your bill-paying and budget work.

➡ *Three Ways to Keep a Computer Checkbook*

1. Write checks and enter them into your check register by hand; record the checks on your computer when the bank statement arrives.

2. Keep the check register on your computer and write checks by hand.

3. Record and print checks on your computer.

This chapter will show you how to do the following:

✔ Record your spending

✔ Build a detailed financial history of your household

In Chapter 3, you will learn how to use this valuable information to gain more control over your spending.

Setting Up Your Accounts

The first step in working with Quicken is to set up your accounts, which are summaries of the financial history you have established based on banking, stocks, and mutual funds. Each account gets its own register. A *register* is a list of all the transactions in the account that Quicken will accurately update each time you correctly add or deduct funds.

When you first install the program, it runs a Setup program that guides you through the process of creating accounts and printing checks. The Setup program can show you how to use the software, step by step. If you're interrupted or don't want to run the Setup program when you first use Quicken, you can always go back later and pick up where you left off. The Setup program can be run at any point while Quicken is running; click on the HomeBase button at the upper-left corner of the screen and the Setup program will appear as one of the options.

Quicken will help you whip your finances into shape, but don't try to do it all at once. Set up each account properly before you tackle the next one. Unless you're willing to devote a full weekend to the process, your first goal should be to set up your checking account. Over time, you can create new accounts for all

➜ *Choosing the Right Version of Quicken*

Quicken can be run on any personal computer, but you need to make sure you have the right version for your system. Quicken is available for DOS, Mac, and Windows, plus there's a deluxe version for Windows only. The deluxe version requires a CD-ROM drive; the others can be loaded onto your hard drive from floppy disks.

Each version provides the same basic set of tools for paying bills, creating a budget, and tracking investments. The deluxe edition adds software for creating a home inventory, updating stock prices, tutorials on learning to use Quicken, a mutual fund selector, and advice from two financial experts—Jane Bryant Quinn and Marshall Loeb.

If you've been thinking about installing Windows on your system, this is as good a time as any because the version of Quicken that runs under Windows is the easiest to use and has more helpful tools than the others. Before you buy Windows, make sure you have available at least 4MB of memory, a graphics adapter, a mouse, and at least 20MB of space on your hard disk.

If your computer has the horsepower, by all means, get the Deluxe version of Quicken 4 for the extra bit of financial advice. While you don't need to have a sound board installed to use the program's other features, one is required to hear the recorded financial advice from the experts.

All of the examples described in this book are based on Quicken 4, though much of it applies to the earlier versions as well. The table below tells you which version of Quicken is appropriate to your computer system

Your Computer	The Right Version
1MB of memory or less	Quicken 8 for DOS
More than 1MB of memory	Quicken 4 Deluxe for Windows on floppy disks
Multimedia system	Quicken 4 Deluxe for Windows on CD-ROM

of your financial dealings, including mutual funds, savings accounts, credit cards, and loans.

If all you want to do is create a budget, you can use Quicken to duplicate the records of your handwritten checkbook, but you'll be making the best use of your time if you also use Quicken to print the checks. You'll enter each transaction just once; the check will be printed and you'll have a permanent record that is linked to all of your other accounts. Reconciling your bank statement will be easier because the computer will do all the math. Once you get the hang of it, you'll actually finish the job of paying bills more quickly.

→ The Quicken Toolbar

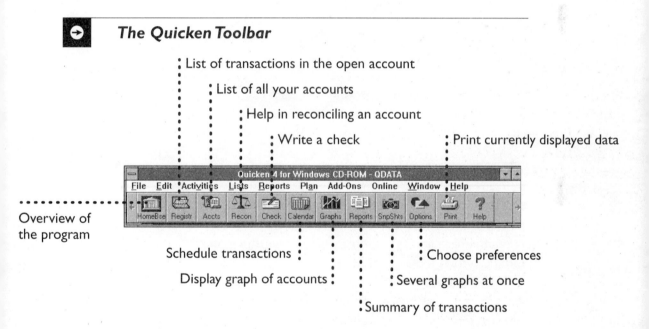

List of transactions in the open account

List of all your accounts

Help in reconciling an account

Write a check

Print currently displayed data

Overview of the program

Schedule transactions

Display graph of accounts

Choose preferences

Several graphs at once

Summary of transactions

If you decide to use Quicken to print your checks, you should order checks the first time you run the program. The Setup program includes an option called Intuit Marketplace that will guide you through the process of ordering checks directly from Quicken's publisher, Intuit. Many other companies sell checks for Quicken at a discount so you may be able to save a little money by ordering checks from another source. However, you may find that the money saved is not worth the extra effort.

➡ *Printing checks one page at a time*

Laser printers and inkjet printers output checks one *page* at a time instead of one *check* at a time as do dot-matrix printers.

Laser printer

Many people have had problems getting their checks to line up properly—especially on dot-matrix printers—and require technical support from Intuit. If you own a dot-matrix printer, you should order checks directly from Intuit to minimize the chance of a problem developing and to increase the likelihood that Intuit can solve it over the phone.

Inkjet and laser printers create output for a single page at a time and they have an easier time printing checks. If you own a laser printer or an inkjet printer, you can feel comfortable about ordering checks from a source other than Intuit.

During the couple of weeks it takes for the check order to be filled (regardless of the source), you'll have to continue paying bills by hand. You don't save any time by ordering from Intuit directly by phone or by modem. Phone and modem orders also require that you mail a check from your current account to ensure that there are no errors when your personalized checks are printed. Be sure to write "void" on the check so no one will be able to write a check on your account. Intuit's check printing service must read the specially coded ink on a real check from your account—a copy won't do.

➔ *Check-Printing Problems*

The most vexing problem you'll encounter with Quicken or any other personal financial program is printing your first batch of checks. For many people, it works the first time, and every time. But others spend hours solving the problems that can crop up.

Here's a checklist of how to solve printing problems fast. For more help, read the file ALIGN.TXT in the directory \CHAPTER.2 under Shareware and More on the companion CD-ROM.

✔ Test the printer with the sample checks you receive. If the checks don't print properly right away, don't proceed until you make xerox copies of the samples to use as you continuing testing.

✔ Make sure you've selected the right type of check by referring to the Check Printer Setup dialog box on the File menu.

✔ Experiment with the check alignment option on the Check Printer Setup dialog box.

✔ Try a different font using the Check Printer Setup dialog box.

✔ Try replacing your printer driver by using the Windows control panel and running the Printers option. If your exact printer isn't listed, select one that's similar. (For example, if you have an Epson laser printer, try an HP laser printer.) If this doesn't fix the problem, change the printer back to the original setting.

✔ Call Quicken's tech support department at 415-858-6085.

While you're ordering checks, also consider ordering window envelopes, too. Because they display the address on your checks through the window, you don't need to write out the address by hand. You only need to type the address of your payees in your check register once. Then, each time you create a check for this payee, the address is automatically printed. This practice also prevents you from introducing errors that could occur when re-entering a payee's address.

If you've just installed Quicken and have started entering new payments, continue to record information about each check as you would with the register in your physical checkbook. You'll gain practice in using Quicken as you develop a sound recordkeeping system that will help you create a feasible budget.

Window envelopes are time savers.

Not only can you save time, but you also avoid introducing errors by entering payee information into the register just once.

Recording Your First Transactions

When you begin the process of using software to create a check register, you can either start with the next check you need to write or you can use a recent bank statement to enter old checks. Try to enter as many old statements as time permits. This approach will provide you with more details to create your budget and establish better records for filing your taxes. When you first use the software, you'll find that it takes about a minute to enter each transaction. Once you get a feel for how Quicken works, and after many of your regular payees have been entered, you'll be able to enter two or three a minute.

When you set up your checking account, the software discourages you from entering transactions until you have the earliest bank statement you plan to record. That's because it wants you to avoid gaps in your recordkeeping. Don't let this deter you from getting started. You can begin with your most recent bank statement and enter those old statements at a later date. When you do get around to this, make sure you don't skip any checks or statements. Any gap in the sequence of checks will wreak havoc on your running balance. This is because the software creates the current balance by starting with the original balance and subtracting or adding all transactions from that starting point. If you miss even a single check or deposit, your balance will be wrong. While you're in the process of entering old statements, the current balance will be wrong, but as long as you're careful to enter every transaction on the statement, you'll have the correct totals when you finish.

If you just don't have the time or patience to enter old bank statements, you can start your account with the current balance—the one you've recorded in your checkbook after writing the most recent check. Then start entering checks either in the check register or by using the Write Checks command on the Activities menu. It will take you longer to create a budget this way but you'll get there eventually.

Paying Bills with Window Envelopes

- Saves the work of writing out envelopes by hand
- Requires extra effort of typing the address into your check register
- Requires the purchase of special envelopes that match the check size
- Be sure to check the payee's address if the payee sends an envelope with the bill

To navigate in Quicken, use the Tab key to move from one field to the next. For example, after you enter the date (or accept the current date), press Tab to move to the check number field. As you complete your first few transactions, be sure to watch what's happening as you enter information in order to become familiar

The Write Checks screen

When you use the Write Checks command, you see a picture of a check and you fill out the check in a manner very similar to using the check register. The main difference is that the Write Checks command lets you enter the address for the payee. You'll want to do this if you plan to use window envelopes for mailing your checks; Quicken prints the address on the check so it can be seen when it's placed in the window envelope.

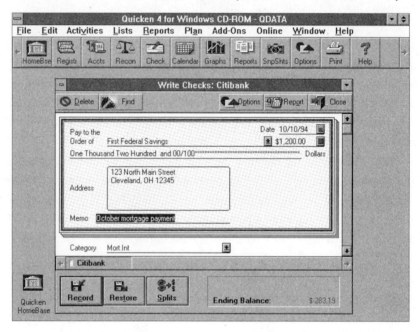

with the program. Periodically, you may notice a little bit of magic after entering your first checks: the more payee names you enter, the more likely it becomes that the payee's name will appear as soon as you type a single letter of the name.

You should also know that Quicken remembers each of your transactions. After you've paid someone once, all of the details about that transaction are added to a list. When you start to type a payee's name on a check, Quicken searches through the list of payees and tries to match that name with the one you're typing. For example, if you've typed "C," the program will immediately insert the name of an old payee that begins with the letter C. Of course, that may not be the

➡ *Using the Tab and Enter Keys in Quicken*

You can end up with a problem if you press Enter in place of Tab and don't catch this mistake. Quicken will automatically complete the check using an amount that may be wrong. You're likely to catch the problem before you mail the check, but you may print it before you catch the error, wasting a check. It may take a little practice, but if you can remember to use the Tab key—rather than Enter—as you complete fields, you won't have the problem. If you do find yourself making this common mistake, be sure to turn off QuickFill.

right name, but Quicken is still ready to help you find the rest of the name. You can type the next letter of the name and Quicken will insert the name of a payee that begins with those two letters; if it's the right name, press the Tab key to accept the name and move on to the amount of the check. If it's still not right, type in the next character, and Quicken inserts the next payee. As soon as you enter the amount of the transaction, the software automatically calculates your new checking balance. This feature is called QuickFill, and after you get the hang of it, you'll feel as if the program is whisking you through the bill-paying process. You can turn off QuickFill if you find it creates problems. To turn off QuickFill, select the Options button at the top of the Register window or the Write Checks window. Once you've opened the Options window, click on Automatic Completion of Fields so the check does not appear in the box. Then select OK to record the change. A common mistake that occurs while QuickFill is on is pressing the Enter key instead of the Tab key once you've entered information into a field; this will complete the transaction in lieu of allowing you to continue working with it.

After you've completed an entire bank statement's worth of checks, you'll be able to take advantage of another time-saving feature: Reconciliation.

Quicken's Reconciliation option will display all of the checks you've written that have not been checked off as cleared. Going through this list, you can quickly compare your own records with those from the bank. This is the time to include transactions that the bank logged in your account, such as adding checking account interest and deducting bank fees. Because Quicken does the math for you, the process of reconciliation can take just a few minutes—and without the headaches it usually causes when done by hand.

● Quicken Quick Entry Tips

● When entering dates, press Tab to use the current date, press the + key to move ahead a day or more, and press the – key to move back.

● When entering old dates, click on the Calendar button and select the date with your mouse.

● When entering a new check that you'll print, type P for the check number (Quicken will assign a number after the check prints).

● When entering checks that will not be printed, press the + key to use the next number in your check series.

● When entering the name of a payee, enter just a couple of letters and see if Quicken has found the correct name. This works in the Category field, too.

Fine-Tuning Your Accounts

Quicken anticipates many of your needs, so for the first few hours you spend with it, make every effort to follow its subtle hints about how to use it. For example, when it suggests you choose a category every time you record a check, it's a good idea to make that effort. This may be the first time you will have recorded categories for your payments but in the long run you'll be glad you started doing it. However, once you've got the basics under your belt, it won't be long before you'll want to customize Quicken to make it reflect the way you have set up your finances.

Quicken excels at remembering which bills need to be paid monthly. To schedule transactions that should be paid on a regular basis, open the Lists menu and select Scheduled Transactions. A dialog box will open that asks for the details. Choose the account and the payee. If you've already recorded a list of transactions, simply select the transaction from the list.

Use the Create Scheduled Transactions dialog box to establish a payment as a regularly recurring item. Quicken will remember to generate a check when the payment is due. If the amount changes from one month to the next, simply enter a new amount. Before long, you'll find that this one feature alone dramatically cuts your bill-paying time.

After you've entered most of your regular bills into your checking account, you can schedule transactions even faster by using the Financial Calendar feature to automate the process of paying bills. When you select Financial Calendar, the screen presents a calendar of the current month. Next to it is a list of any account you wish to see, though the most common choice is your checking account.

To pay a check on a certain day, move your mouse until it points to the correct payee, and then click on the name. Next, hold the left mouse button down and drag the name to the correct date. Quicken will open a dialog box of options so you can confirm that this transaction should be memorized for the date you've selected.

 ### *Paying bills by Calendar*

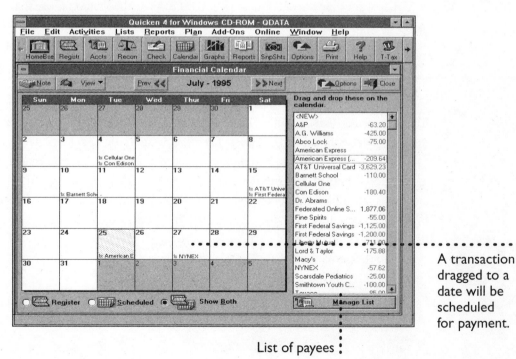

A transaction dragged to a date will be scheduled for payment.

List of payees

This feature can be used for most of your bills, even those that have a different amount each month, such as an electric bill. The check will not be generated until you open Quicken on or after that date. Then you have the opportunity to change the amount and review the transaction before you choose the option of printing the check. There are several options for controlling how Quicken will record this payment, including whether you will be prompted for the amount or whether the last amount should be used to make the next payment.

Managing Quicken Data Files

Unlike some other software programs, Quicken automatically names your data files and routinely saves your data to a file. Normally, you never have to think about the data file, except when Quicken periodically reminds you to make a backup copy. In addition to keeping the backup copy you'll use in case of a loss, you may want to make an extra copy so you can use the data on more than one computer. To place your data files on a floppy disk, open Quicken's File menu and select the Export command. You can also use a file management program such as Windows File Manager to copy to a disk every file in the Quicken directory that begins with QDATA. When you want to use this data on another computer that is running Quicken, you can either use the File menu's Restore command to access the data, or you can copy the QDATA files into the Quicken directory. Copying the files will overwrite the QDATA files that are already in the Quicken directory.

If you want to use Quicken data files in other applications, you'll need to use the Export command on the File menu to save the file in a text format. Quicken accounts use a file format called QIF (Quicken Interchange Format) that can be read by any program that uses ASCII text. For help in understanding this file format, read the file QIF.TXT in the directory \CHAPTER.2 under Shareware and More on the companion CD-ROM.

Building a Spreadsheet Check Register

If you'd rather not spend $50 on Quicken, you can use any spreadsheet to manage your checkbook. It's not a difficult task; setting up the spreadsheet should take

Making sense of a QIF file

Tax preparation programs like TaxCut can read QIF files directly. However, setting up other financial software programs can require extensive work if the program does not directly read the QIF format. If you're going to use QIF files to do your own analysis on a spreadsheet, you'll need to set up a translation table in your work.

A data file that contains these tables and explains how to set up other programs to work with the QIF format is on the CD-ROM that comes with this book. The Quicken manual has details on how to use the QIF format.

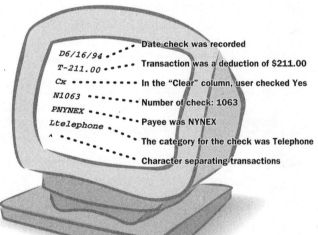

```
D6/16/94  ........  Date check was recorded
T-211.00  ........  Transaction was a deduction of $211.00
Cx        ........  In the "Clear" column, user checked Yes
N1063     ........  Number of check: 1063
PNYNEX    ........  Payee was NYNEX
Ltelephone ......  The category for the check was Telephone
^         ........  Character separating transactions
```

an experienced computer user less time than installing Quicken. The advantage to using a spreadsheet to manage your check register—aside from the $50 you'll save if you already own a spreadsheet—is the ability to store your transactions in a format that allows for infinite levels of customization.

The disadvantage to using a spreadsheet is you'll still have to write checks by hand and the spreadsheet will not be full of the many tricks that Quicken provides, such as scheduling recurring transactions, cross-referencing checks between accounts, and creating budget reports.

The easiest way to create a spreadsheet checkbook is to use your current check register as a model with one exception: In the first row, keep a calculation for the balance. Use one cell in the first row to label the balance and in the next cell, enter this formula (which can be used in either Microsoft Works or Microsoft Excel):

=(SUM(G3:G1001))-((SUM(D3:D1001))+(SUM(F3:F1001)))

Doing it yourself with a spreadsheet

Set up your spreadsheet so that payments are recorded in column D, fees in column F, and deposits in column G. The formula =(SUM(G3:G1001))-((SUM(D3:D1001))+(SUM(F3:F1001))) will total all deposits, total all debits (payments and fees), and then subtract the debits from the deposits. This calculation gives you the current balance.

	A	B	C	D	E	F	G	H
1			Balance	$633.14				
2								
	Check no.	Date	Description of Transaction	Payment	?	Fees	Deposit	Category
3			2/1/95 Opening Balance				$1,000.00	
4	101	2/2/95	J.C. Penney	$50.00				clothing
5	102	2/3/95	Alphabet Land	$100.00				childcare
6			2/5/95 Paycheck -- Joe's				$975.88	
7	103	2/5/95	A&P	$115.23				food
8	104	2/5/95	VISA	$865.44				credit card
9	105	2/5/95	Bell Atlantic	$112.08				utility -- phone
10	106	2/5/95	Con Edison	$88.45				utility -- electric
11			2/10/95 Paycheck -- Ann's				$1,024.33	
12	107	2/12/95	Bill & Jane Gordon	$100.00				gift
13	108	2/15/95	Barnes & Noble	$55.43				books
14			2/1/595 checking charge			$15.00		
15	109	2/1/5/95	American Express	$865.44				credit card
16								
17								
18								
19								
20								
21								
22								

A spreadsheet-checkbook is included on the companion CD-ROM; you'll find it in the directory \CHAPTER.3 under Worksheets. To start entering checks, record the opening balance on row 3. Then begin to record each check that you write. Every time an amount is entered in the payment, fees, or deposit columns, the balance will be updated. After you've entered more checks than will fit on the screen, you should use the Split screen command on the Window menu so you can see the balance and column headings at all times.

As long as you're taking the time to enter all of your checks, it's a good idea to put every payment into a category, such as clothing, food, or entertainment, for example. Even if you don't track all payments, make a note for checks that are tax-deductible, such as property taxes, and charitable contributions. To do this, you can either create a category called "Tax-Deductible," or you could create one called "T" where you record tax-deductible items.

When you want to find all of the checks in a particular category, sort the spreadsheet using the Category column as the sort key. To do this in Microsoft Works, highlight the cells that are part of the checkbook (everything except the headings and balance). Then, choose the Select Rows command on the Tools menu. In the dialog box that opens, enter H (or whichever column you're using for categories) as the first column to be sorted. Select OK and the checks will be listed alphabetically by category.

All of the checks in a particular category, such as charity or tax-deductible payment, will be grouped together. To return the spreadsheet to its layout as a checkbook register, sort the rows again using column B (the date) as the first column to be sorted and column A (the check number) as the second column.

Ready for the Future

Each year, the maintenance of paper records gives way to electronic recordkeeping systems. For example, now that financial organizations have made electronic banking available to their customers, it's only a matter of time before all checking accounts and credit card records will be available in electronic form. However, it's still too early to know how this will happen. Maybe you'll receive a floppy disk in the mail with your statements or maybe your computer will make a modem connection. Or maybe you'll receive the data in an electronic form not yet invented. But all leading banks are actively exploring ways to deliver financial records in computer-readable form. Some banks have already started to offer home banking. Right now, these services do little beyond what Quicken provides; you're able to move money between accounts and write checks. One of the advantages is protection against check bouncing, since the bank software will not let you overdraw your account. But the bank software is likely to be difficult to use and doesn't have extra features to help you use the account information, such as recording categories for payments. One of the easiest ways to begin using electronic banking right now is to sign up with one of the banks offering services through the Prodigy online service. You must be a subscriber to Prodigy, and you must open an account with one of the banks offering services through Prodigy. To find out more, when you're logged into Prodigy, type the jumpword "banking." While Quicken is hoping to work out arrangements providing compatibility between Quicken files and online banks, as of this writing, using a bank online requires keeping separate records in the bank software and in your Quicken files.

> *It's only a matter of time before all checking accounts and credit card records will be available in electronic form.*

Today, you have the option of being on the cutting edge of technology in two ways. You can use a credit card offered by Quicken that will provide you with your monthly statement on a floppy disk. That saves you from the work of entering each credit card transaction into your Quicken accounts. Or, you can pay bills electronically by using the CheckFree bill-paying service. To set up an account, select the CheckFree option on the Activities submenu of Quicken's Main menu. Once the account is open, you use your computer's modem to send a file directly to CheckFree's computer. This spares you from printing and mailing checks. Then, CheckFree will take responsibility for making the payment electronically.

In reality, the American economy is not yet ready for electronic funds transfers. Only about half of all the payments sent to CheckFree in 1994 were paid electronically. While large corporations are prepared to receive payments this way, many small businesses are not. For these payments, CheckFree's computers print paper checks and mail them, the same as you would do with the same risk of having the check lost in the mail. Additionally, because the CheckFree payment cannot include the printed statement you received with your original bill, it's quite possible it will take even longer for a CheckFree payment to be cleared. Finally, some people like the convenience of maintaining a paperless office in their home and using CheckFree does accomplish that goal. But unfortunately, it does not yet offer the certainty of knowing that a payment will be made exactly on the date you want it to be made.

Keep in mind that the effort of setting up check registers and recording all of your checks on your computer is a valuable component in a forward-thinking financial strategy. Here's a list of some of the long-term benefits of using Quicken:

- Doing less work at tax time if checks are categorized
- Knowing exactly where your money went
- Having easy access to permanent records of all payments that can be analyzed by category

This means for now, you'll be making a smart investment of time if you record all of your checks in a Quicken account and print computer checks. Then, stay informed about changing technology. Someday, electronic funds transfers will be a practical way to pay bills. In the meantime, the data files you're building will only become more valuable, regardless of the future direction of digital technology.

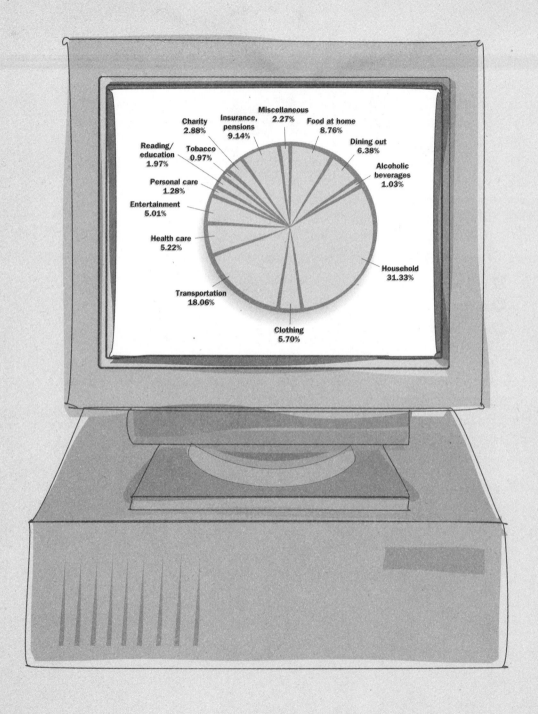

3

Trimming the Fat

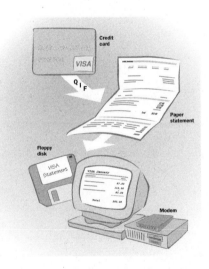

40 Let Quicken Do Your Budget

42 Adjusting Categories to Reflect Spending

44 Tracking Your Cash

46 Making Credit Cards Work for You

50 Shopping for Value Online

Could

you cut your spending? Of course you could. You don't need to eat in restaurants. You don't need to buy new clothes as often as you do. You could spend a lot less and still live comfortably. In fact, you can probably think of a hundred ways to spend less. But of course, you don't want to cut back. You want to have a good income and enjoy owning the things you've earned.

There are no firm rules on how much a person like you should spend on clothes, food, and shelter. However, there is a limit and it's equal to your income. If you're smart, you'll spend less than that and put aside some money for the future. But no matter how much you're spending and saving, you'll do a better job at each task if you occasionally create a budget that accurately reflects how you're spending money.

The process of creating a budget is not just about making ends meet. It should get you to think about how you're spending your money. After you've seen the general breakdown, you'll be in a better position to make decisions about your future. For example, you'll be able to realistically answer the following question: Are you saving enough?

Most experts advise a savings rate of between 5 and 10 percent of annual income. One immediate reason to put money aside is to create a big enough cushion so you could survive losing your job. Experts agree that the search for a new job can take four or five months and you should be prepared to live off your savings while you search. So two of the most immediate benefits of creating a budget are seeing if you have enough money set aside for a rainy day and determining how much you absolutely must spend to maintain living in your current home, driving your car and carrying on while you look for a new job.

A budget helps you look at your spending from a different perspective. For example, a budget will clearly show you that mortgage payments, rent, utilities, medical expenses, and groceries are not the only necessities. Household repairs, insurance premiums and car maintenance are also essential. But entertainment, dining, and gifts are discretionary (you can probably even think of a few more). Furthermore, categorizing expenses reveals a lot about your lifestyle. For instance, you probably don't spend a lot of time thinking about whether dinner in a restaurant is entertainment or food, but doing a budget forces you to make that choice. If you're dining out simply to eat, you may want to devise cheaper ways to have your meals. If you consider dining out a form of entertainment and your other entertainment expenses are low, restaurants may represent good value for you. Most people spend close to 5 percent of their income on entertainment.

How Americans spend their money

The process of budgeting will force you to think about your finances differently. Adopting this new point of view will make a wealth of valuable information available to you. For example, if you realize that mortgage payments take up about half of your income, you'll have good reason to feel strapped for cash; the average American spends only about one-third of his or her income on housing. You'll probably find that your spending patterns aren't too far from the national averages.

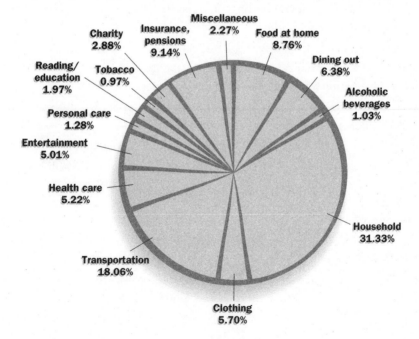

This chapter will show you how to do the following:

✔ Use Quicken to set up a budget

✔ Create pie charts and bar charts to display financial data

✔ Track cash payments

✔ Use credit cards wisely

✔ Consult online forums and bulletin boards for product information

Let Quicken Do Your Budget

Whether you pay all of your bills with Quicken, record data in Quicken while you continue to write checks by hand, or record checking transactions in a spreadsheet, after a few months, you'll have all the facts needed to have your computer calculate a budget.

Quicken can help you set up a budget based on your estimates of what you should spend in each category. A better strategy is to let the computer do the work by creating a budget that uses real transactions from your accounts. All you need to do is select the Activities menu, choose Set Up Budgets, and select Auto. Quicken is now ready to automatically set up a budget based on the transactions you've recorded. It will prompt you for the specific months it should use for the budget. Once you've entered a period of time, the program displays a report that shows how much money you've spent in every category (based on how you identified each transaction) and compares it to your income. At the bottom of the report is the important number: the difference between inflow and outflow. If you see a negative number, you're probably building up debt because you're spending more than you're earning. If you see a positive number here, this is what you have left over and you should be able to save it. Many people will end up with a positive number but won't be able to find a surplus in their checking account; this means you haven't recorded all of your spending. The culprit is most likely cash withdrawals that you didn't record.

The list of figures may be difficult to grasp, so try a graphical presentation. Click on the Graphs button and Quicken will display these figures as charts. A pie chart shows how all of your spending breaks down into percentages over the

Looking at Spending by Categories

Quicken can help you set up a budget based on your estimates of what you should spend in each category. A better strategy is to let the computer do the work by creating a budget that uses real transactions from your accounts. All you need to do is select the Activities menu, choose Set Up Budgets, and select Auto.

Quicken 4 for Windows CD-ROM - QDATA								

File Edit Activities Lists Reports Plan Add-Ons Online Window Help

Accts Cat List Registr Recon Check Print Graphs Reports Calendar Prefs UseAcct Help Q-Quote Q-Tax Inventry Port

Budget

Create Edit ▼ Layout Print Save Restore Close

Category View	Jan	Feb	Mar	Apr	May	June	July	Totals
⊟ **INFLOWS**								
└ ◆ Salary	3680	3680	3680	3680	3680	3680	3680	44160
⊟ **OUTFLOWS**								
Auto	-85	-99	-114	-68	-111	-45	-87	-1034
Bank Chrg	-15	-15	-15	-15	-15	-15	-15	-180
Childcare	-250	-250	-290	-250	-250	-250	-250	-2040
Clothing	-150	-150	-220	-500	-650	-150	0	-1820
Dining	-120	-145	-87	-150	-86	-104	-125	-1417
Entertain	-55	-112	-67	-52	-43	-109	-55	-1243
Groceries	-411	-376	-417	-298	-401	-421	-355	-4679
Home Rpair	-105	-11	0	0	-215	0	0	-831
Household	-64	-23	-55	-45	-22	-87	-54	-1350
Insurance	-71	-71	-71	-71	-71	-71	-71	-852
Landscaping	0	0	0	-125	-125	-125	-125	-795
Medical	-50	0	-115	-15	0	0	-225	-415
Mort Int	-1565	-1565	-1565	-1565	-1565	-1565	-1565	-18780
School Tuition	-150	-150	-150	-150	-150	-150	0	-900
Telephone	-63	-87	-117	-75	-65	-88	-87	-897
Utilities	-128	-143	-118	-87	-78	-74	-71	-1339
Total Inflows	3680	3680	3680	3680	3680	3680	3680	44160
Total Outflows	-3282	-3197	-3401	-3466	-3947	-3254	-3085	-38572
Difference	398	483	279	214	-167	426	595	5588

entire period you specified. A bar chart shows income and expenses each month for the entire period. This snapshot shows you where your money is going and which times of year you may have gotten yourself into trouble with overspending. It may also point out gaps in your recordkeeping.

The first time you create a budget based on real spending, many of your totals are likely to be less than the real amounts by quite a lot. This number will only be correct if you've been religiously tracking every transaction for a long time, including cash that you've spent. As you examine the budget report, you'll probably spot problems in the categories. Dining, for example, may not reflect all of the meals you've eaten outside the home. To get a truly accurate budget, you need to carefully look at the figures in each category and ask yourself if they "sound" correct. After you've done some detective work, you can use these budget figures as a guide to control your spending.

If you're considering a large purchase, open up the budget and try playing with the numbers. How badly would a stereo purchase hurt the bottom line? Could you pay for it if you cut back on dining and clothing for the next two months? Quicken will recalculate the totals to show you the effects of changing your spending habits. If you find a combination that you'd like to strive for, print a copy as a reference point. Don't rely on your memory because human nature is likely to make you err on the side of optimism; a black-and-white copy of the budget will help you remember that your new toy will be paid for by cutting those dining and clothing expenses.

Adjusting Categories to Reflect Spending

Displaying a budget for the first time will most likely be an incentive to go over your accounts and edit the categories that have been recorded for each transaction. You'll want to make sure the categories more accurately reflect the way you've been spending your money. The easiest way to review your categories is to open up your checking register and review each transaction, asking yourself if the category selected for each is the best choice.

A more advanced technique for examining how you've assigned categories is to generate a report for all of the transactions in that category and to review the category as a whole. This way, you'll be able to see all of the transactions in that category at once. To do this, select Categories & Transfers from the Lists menu. Scroll through this list until you find the category that you want to understand better. Once you've highlighted this category, click on the Report button. A window will open that shows all transactions in the category. See the table below for guidelines on appropriate entries for various categories.

If you see a transaction that seems out of place, you can change it easily by using the Zoom feature that is available when a report is open. As you move your cursor over the transaction, the cursor changes to a magnifying glass with a

Take Care with Confusing Budget Categories

Categories	Entries
Entertainment	Includes both in-home recreation such as video rentals and "night-out" activities such as movies and bowling
Dining	All restaurants, including fast food and take-out, but not groceries
Clothing	Break into separate categories for each family member

Z in the center. If you double-click the mouse or press Enter while this magnifying glass is resting on a transaction, Quicken will open the register where this transaction was recorded. You can then edit the category and record the change. Quicken will change the recorded transaction immediately, so if you close the account register and return to the report window, you'll see the change has already taken place.

Your budget does not have to be absolutely accurate to be valuable. While some of your transactions such as mortgage and rent can be accurately projected, other expenses (electric bills, phone bills) will be estimates. If you've just started using Quicken recently and haven't recorded dozens of transactions, you can still create a realistic budget and, at the same time, set up your accounts to make bill-paying easier. The trick is to create a scheduled transaction for every regular bill and source of income (the process was described in Chapter 2, in the section "Fine-Tuning Your Accounts"). Creating the scheduled transactions by using a recent bill allows you to base your projection on a real world figure. That's a far better way to build a budget than guessing about what you should be spending. If you're uncomfortable using approximate amounts, the solution is to go back and enter the data on last year's checking statements. Your budget can then be based on average amounts paid in each category over the last year.

Not all of the problems with the budget report are based on recording payments to the wrong category. Some of the problems will stem from "umbrella" transactions, which hide specific expenses. For example, the Auto category will be too low if it doesn't include gas purchases. You can safely project gas purchases for the purposes of the budget using recent history as a guide.

If you're trying to get spending under control, identify as many items as possible and try to get specific. Don't assign all meal purchases to the category of Dining. Use the Category & Lists command to set up new subcategories under Dining, like Breakfast, Snacks, and Lunch. This technique gives you the option of seeing all dining expenses broken down within one total. You don't have to make a recording of every trip to the soda machine at work but if you know that about half of the cash you withdrew was spent on meals at work, go ahead and enter that amount as an estimate.

Once you've gotten very specific, Quicken can help you take a broader view so you can see the big picture. It provides a function for grouping categories as super-categories. To set up a super-category, select the Edit menu when the Budget window is open. Quicken will present a list of all categories and let you create a super-category that allows you to group similar categories. This gives you a different perspective on spending without removing the convenience of tracking spending in each category. For example, job-related expenses such as commuting tickets, special clothes, and meals eaten at work could be grouped into a super-category. You tell Quicken to display the super-category groupings by selecting the Layout button on the Budget menu.

Tracking Your Cash

Getting specific is easy when you're recording checks. But the two biggest sources of budget gaps for new Quicken users are the topics of this section and the next one: cash spending and credit card payments. If you're happy with the results of your budget so far, you may not need to take the next two steps. But if you really want to get spending under control, you'll have to start tracking cash and splitting up credit card payments into finer detail.

Life is short and spending cash may be one of the few pleasures you have left, so don't burden it with too many stipulations. One of the most important reasons to track cash spending is to record items that may be tax-deductible. Tax planners report that cash spent on volunteer work is one of the most commonly overlooked deductions. While you can't deduct the cost of filling up your tank just because you're driving to do volunteer work, you can deduct mileage (at

12 cents a mile), parking charges, or any other expense incurred while you were helping an IRS-recognized charitable organization. If you slip a few dollars into a church collection box, you should keep a record by assigning some of the cash to the Charity category. When it comes time to file your federal return, it will be a lot easier to summarize donations if you've kept this kind of record.

If you use an ATM to withdraw cash from your checking account, you'll need to record the transactions in order to reconcile your checking records with the bank's so it's smart to record all cash withdrawals in a Quicken register. Besides, people who reconcile their checking accounts say that banks do make mistakes that you'll only catch by performing this frequently ignored chore.

> *One of the most important reasons to track cash spending is to record items that may be tax-deductible.*

You can keep your accounts up to date by saving the withdrawal and deposit receipts and entering them individually. Or you can wait until the bank statement arrives and do it on a monthly basis. Of course, if you don't save your receipts, you'll lose the ability to keep tabs on the bank if you have only their records and none of your own. As long as you're entering the withdrawals, why not try to identify at least some of the directions in which your cash has headed?

You can use Quicken to track cash spending in two different ways. The easiest method is to enter deductions from your bank accounts as cash withdrawals. The more sophisticated technique is to set up a cash account that lists every cash withdrawal separately. Using a cash account takes more work because you have to switch over to it every time you want to record a transaction instead of listing it along with the checks. And you have to do a little more work at the keyboard because you have to identify the source of the money. If you usually withdraw money from your checking account, it's a bit less work to stick with the checking register for your cash withdrawals. If you withdraw money from both a savings and a checking account, it's a good idea to create a cash account.

Using either method, you can allocate the money to a category, such as clothing, dining, or miscellaneous. In most cases, no single category will do justice to the myriad ways in which you've decided to spend the dollars. But you can try, using the Splits feature. By clicking on the Splits button when recording the cash withdrawal, you can assign the money into any of your spending categories.

You'll probably find that splitting up cash payments raises the possibility of countless new categories: haircuts, junk food, you name it. If you discover items you spend money on often, you may want to create new categories that make it easy for you to record them. But don't get carried away and create too many categories. Money spent at McDonald's is probably best identified as a dining expense no matter how ironic that may seem.

Making Credit Cards Work for You

A common mistake in trying to get on a budget is seeing credit cards as the problem—"If I didn't use this card, I'd be okay" goes the popular lament. Remember, credit cards may lead to frivolous purchases because they're easier to use than a check, but cash is even easier to spend. Focusing on credit cards as villains ignores the fact that the proper use of a credit card can be a very smart way to spend your money, as long as you pay the bill in full each month.

It can't be stressed enough that using a credit card without paying off the monthly balance is a mistake. When you keep a running balance on your credit card, you're paying interest at one of the highest rates around; it's the worst way imaginable to pay bills. Using a credit card to get you through a transition in your life, such as furnishing a new home or settling into a new city, is perhaps the only good reason to maintain credit card debt. Just don't let the debt from the transition last for too long.

If you use your credit card only as a way of shifting payment methods and you pay your bill in full every month, you're using one of the smartest ways available to pay bills. Regular use of a credit card creates a written record of your spending and it will help you increase your net worth over time because you'll enjoy the interest you can earn on delayed credit card payments. Here's how it works. Every time you buy something with a credit card, you're able to keep the money in your checking account until the credit card bill becomes due. That means, on average, you have 30 extra days to use the money. In small doses, that's no big deal. With typical savings and checking account interest rates of

5 percent, holding on to a $100 for an extra month saves you about 33 cents. But if you carefully manage your money so that you keep only what's needed in your checking account with the rest earning higher interest rates, you can earn a good bit more. If you do this regularly, the savings will start to add up.

➡ *Adding up the little gains*

This example shows that, over the course of a year, someone who used a credit card for $8,750 worth of purchases would end up gaining about $73 from aggressively investing the money that would have otherwise been spent by paying bills in cash. If you were conservative and kept the money in a low interest bearing account that earned 5 percent, the gain would be about $36. The point is, don't be afraid to use a credit card if you can make it work for you.

```
Microsoft Works
File  Edit  View  Insert  Format  Tools  Window  Help
Arial          10         B / U  Σ $
A20
                          CRCD_SAV.WK1
        A              B                    C                D    E
```

Annual gain from paying by credit card without paying interest

	Monthly credit card charges	Amount gained from the float*
January	$750	$6.25
February	$500	$4.17
March	$500	$4.17
April	$750	$6.25
May	$1,000	$8.33
June	$750	$6.25
July	$500	$4.17
August	$750	$6.25
September	$500	$4.17
October	$1,000	$8.33
November	$750	$6.25
December	$1,000	$8.33
Total	**$8,750**	**$72.92**

*-- based on investing the amount incurred for credit charges for 30 days and getting a 10 percent return on the investment

```
Press ALT to choose commands, or F2 to edit                    NUM
```

I created a simple spreadsheet to demonstrate the effect of investing money that was freed up by using a credit card. (You'll find this spreadsheet on the companion CD-ROM in CR_CDSAV.WK1 in the directory \CHAPTER.3 under Worksheets.

You can open it with either Microsoft Works, Lotus 1-2-3, Microsoft Excel—a version is available for each program.) Using Microsoft Works, I entered an approximate credit card bill for 12 months. Then, I set out to estimate how much this money would earn if it were invested for 30 days instead of paid right away. The spreadsheet formula IPMT (for interest payment) calculates the amount of interest that an investment will return. I used a 10 percent investment return as the interest rate (that's the average return from investing in stocks over the last 65 years). The formula assumes that each credit card bill is delayed by 30 days; on average, that's about how much time you have to defer credit card charges. Some credit card charges are posted by a store within days and others take weeks.

The proper use of a credit card can be a very smart way to spend your money.

Heavy use of a credit card may help you grow your cash position but it can lead to poor record documentation. Each credit card transaction represents many small purchases and if your checking account register simply notes the credit card payment, you'll have no idea of what you bought. After all, you're not buying a credit card, you're buying clothing, meals, and services with the card payment. It's important to make sure you keep track of individual credit card expenses.

Use the Splits feature in a Quicken check register to allocate all of the specific purchases to individual categories. To get an accurate record of your expenses, you need to go through the itemized bill that comes with your credit card statement. Then use the Splits feature to list each item separately. Fortunately, the Splits feature makes this process easy. When you're entering transactions in your check register, you can click on the Splits feature to open a "mini-register" that lets you identify each of the credit card purchases. As you enter each amount, Quicken calculates how much of the statement amount is left. If the purchases you've entered add up to the statement total, Quicken confirms that the entry is properly divided. If there's a discrepancy, you can resolve it by either changing the amount of the payment recorded or by entering the difference as an unidentified charge. There shouldn't be anything left over; if there are finance charges being paid, be sure to identify them.

Split large transactions into categories

The Splits feature lets you allocate specific expenses to particular categories. You can open a "mini-register" that lets you identify each item on your credit card.

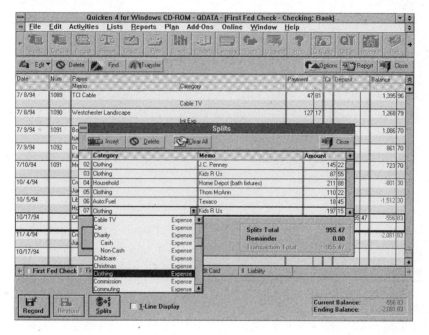

This isn't the only way to itemize credit card bills. Quicken has a more comprehensive solution. You can create a register that will track all activity in your credit card account. Most people won't need to track credit cards with such great detail. However, if you're trying to pay off a balance, this is a good way to help you monitor the account closely and move toward the goal of bringing credit card spending under control.

You record payments in a credit card register the same way you create a check register—by using an opening balance from the current statement. You then enter each purchase in your credit card account using receipts that you receive when you've made a purchase. When you pay the monthly bill, transfer money between the check and credit card registers.

If you're diligent enough to record each charge, you'll end up with an accurate indicator of your next credit card bill. You'll often be pleasantly surprised to find that some charges have not been posted in time to make the next bill. You'll also be able to catch any incorrect billings as soon as you compare your mailed statement to your Quicken register.

Shopping for Value Online

Now that you've taken a good look at how you've been spending your money, let's take a look at how you can plan to be a better consumer. With a modem attached to your computer, you have access to many databases that can help you do research on large purchases before you make your selection.

Consumer Reports is well respected for evaluating products and guiding consumers toward good values. But unless you've got a photographic memory, subscribing to the publication is no guarantee that you'll have the help you need when you're ready to make a purchase. If *Consumer Reports* reviewed something three months ago, how will you find the report if you're planning to shop for a particular item tomorrow?

Articles from *Consumer Reports* are available from the major online services—America Online, CompuServe, and Prodigy. Only Prodigy has a complete listing; the other two services have a more limited selection of certain categories, such as cars and electronics.

Finding Consumer Reports Online

➜ On America Online, use the keyword CONSUMER for recent reports on cars, electronics, home/workshop, and financial products

➜ On CompuServe, type GO CSR for recent reports on cars and electronics

➜ On Prodigy, type the jumpword CONSUMER REPORTS for all recent reports

If you're buying a car, don't venture near a showroom until you've used Auto-Net. Second only to the purchase of a home, buying a car is the single largest

→ Quicken's Intellicharge Service

If the idea of tracking credit card charges this carefully appeals to you, you'll want to try Quicken's Intellicharge service. It's a VISA credit card that prepares your statements in Quicken format that you either download by modem or receive in the mail on a floppy disk.

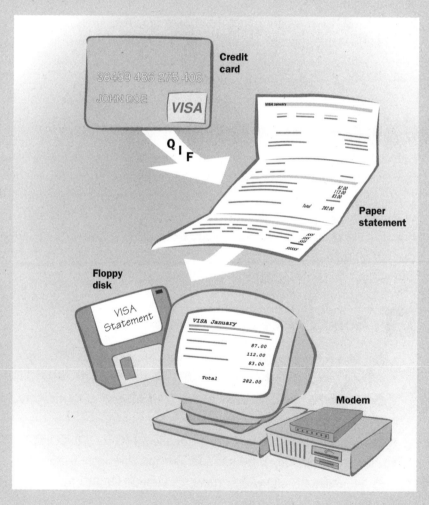

and most complicated expenditure for the average consumer. Not only do you have to haggle with the dealer on the purchase price, you've also got to choose among option packages that may force you to accept frivolous features, such as an automatic antenna when all you want is anti-lock braking. You can save yourself hundreds of dollars by checking AutoNet, a database provided on CompuServe and Prodigy. AutoNet has exactly the kind of information you want to have in hand before walking into the showroom. Most important is the dealer invoice cost—the price the car dealer has to pay to the manufacturer. A good negotiator will ignore the suggested retail price of the car and insist on making a deal for only 7 to 10 percent above this number.

AutoNet reports list figures on 44 specs (including headroom, engine displacement, and steering diameter) and the availability of 31 different options (ranging from power windows to leather seats). The reports are displayed in text only and you can download them onto your system. If you're comparing two or more models, you may want to import the individual reports into a spreadsheet.

An online account can also make you a better consumer by giving you access to a wide circle of other consumers. All online services have forums or bulletin boards (BBs, or BBSs, for bulletin board systems) where people congregate and discuss topics of special interest. Products such as audio equipment, computers, gardening, and sports equipment are all well represented.

➡ Good Places to Ask Online

➡ Cars & Motorcycles BB on Prodigy (Jump to CARSBBS) for buying and fixing cars

➡ Consumer Electronics forum on CompuServe (GO CEFORUM) for buying audio and video equipment

➡ Consumers Plus forum on CompuServe (GO CONSUMER+) for problems with shoddy products and unresponsive manufacturers

➡ Homelife BB on Prodigy (Jump to HOMELIFE BB) for questions on home furnishings and gardening.

➡ MISC.INVEST (an Internet newsgroup) for questions about financial products

➡ *Good Places to Ask Online*

➡ Money Talk BB on Prodigy (Jump to MONEY TALK BB) for questions on investments and bank services

➡ REC.GARDENS (an Internet newsgroup) for questions on gardening and landscaping

➡ ZiffNet on CompuServe (GO ZNT) for using computers, hardware, and software

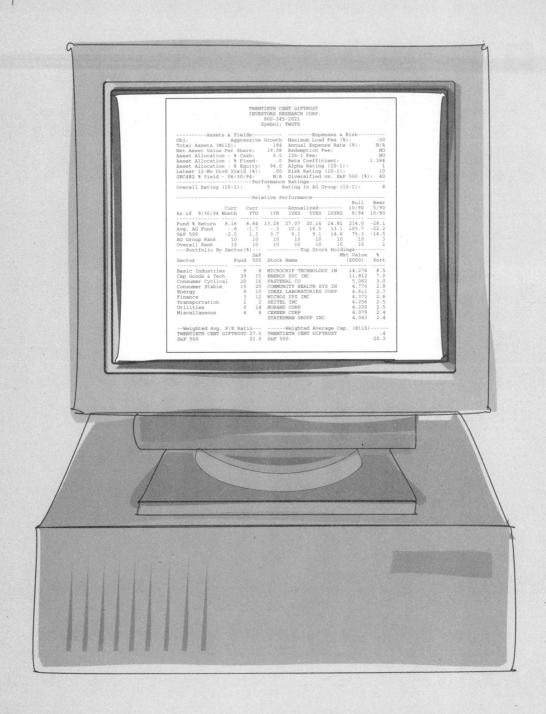

4

Investing Wisely:
Mutual Funds

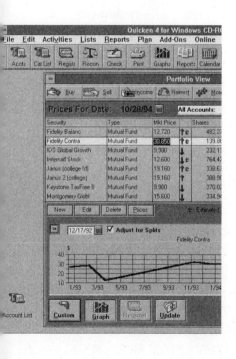

56 Mutual Fund Basics

61 Choosing a Fund Strategy

63 Shopping for Mutual Funds Online

69 Keeping Track of Your Funds

If you haven't yet explored mutual funds, you're missing out on what may be the best investment opportunity available to the average American. Mutual funds have paid off handsomely for average investors in recent years, compiling track records that many successful stock brokers could envy. With as little as $500, you can transform your nest egg from a slow growing bank account into a rapidly growing portfolio that holds a small piece of the most successful companies in the world. Some financial experts contend that the typical American needs to invest in mutual funds to ensure a healthy financial future. With inflation eating up the return from savings bank accounts and CDs, mutual funds are the safest way to share in the wealth created by the stock and bond markets.

Not every mutual fund will deliver double-digit growth. Some funds are designed to avoid risk and as a result, they tend to grow at the relatively slow rate of 6 to 8 percent a year. Fortunately, it's not hard to uncover the differences between funds, and a personal computer with a modem can help you do your own research very quickly.

This chapter will help you understand the nature of mutual funds, the choices you'll encounter in choosing a fund, and the tools on your computer that will help you make the smartest choices.

Mutual Fund Basics

Mutual funds have been around since 1924. For much of that time, investors knew little about how the funds operated, and financial planners quietly sold these funds. But now they are actively marketed to the general public and the smallest details about a fund's operation are open to inspection. Many funds have grown into large companies that manage billions of dollars in assets and provide a wide choice of funds. Fidelity Investments, T. Rowe Price, Vanguard Group, and Dreyfus are a few examples of some companies whose names may be familiar to you.

Here's the principle behind mutual funds: To increase the value of your investments you must take risks, but you can prevent financial disaster by spreading the risk around. A successful mutual fund stategy is based on diversification, or buying shares of many offerings. When any one investment does badly, you lose only a portion of your money. The losses will be balanced by gains from investments that rise in value. Unlike savings bank accounts, mutual funds are not insured by the government so there is a small chance of losing everything. But if you invest with well established companies and you avoid the temptation to sell when the market is down, the risk of losing money is slight.

Mutual Funds Are Sold in Two Ways

- Closed-end funds are not widely traded and are sold through brokers and financial planners. They cannot be researched online.

- Open-end funds are publicly traded. Shares are bought directly from the mutual fund management company or through a financial institution. Information about open-end funds is available online.

In a free-market economy, publicly traded stocks and bonds go through cycles of growth and decline, so a mutual fund has the odds on its side. There's nothing mysterious about how you make money; if you pay attention to market conditions and the reasons why the market is moving, you'll be able to buy stocks and bonds cheaply and sell them after they rise in value. Clearly, a fund's performance is tied to how well its managers perform in trading. They must be quick enough to buy at low prices. A smart investor will take the time to research funds to make sure you're getting the best performing funds. Every mutual fund is guided by a strategy that limits the fund to a specific type of investment and defines the amount of risk it will incur. By choosing among funds, you can create a well rounded portfolio that will take advantage of promising growth areas while keeping some of your money in tried-and-true money-makers.

Conservative investors should start with bond funds. Government bonds are among the most secure investments possible because the U.S. government has never missed a payment and the bonds always pay interest through the full term. The return on corporate bonds tends to be less predictable because bonds issued by corporations are often *called* when interest rates rise, meaning the bond issuer decides it doesn't like the terms of the deal any more. When a bond is called,

A Mutual Fund Sampler

Money market	Buys only CDs and government bonds.
Bond	Buys only corporate and government bonds, typically of a particular type. A bond fund usually specializes in either short- or long-term bonds.
Income	Specializes in the stocks of companies that pay dividends and may also buy corporate bonds.
Growth and Income	Tries to achieve a mixture of dividend paying stocks and companies with growth potential.
Convertible	Buys only stocks and bonds that have been issued as preferred and can be converted to common stock.
International equity	Invests in the stock of foreign companies. Usually specializes in either a region or a single stock market.
Sector	Buys only the stocks of companies in a single industry, such as banking, technology, or real estate.
Small company	Buys only companies below a specified size, hoping to achieve strong growth as the companies mature.

➔ Comparing the Return from Stocks and Bonds

Stocks have more ups and downs than bonds but over time stocks provide higher returns.

	20 Years	10 Years	5 Years
Stocks	12.2%	14.8%	15.1%
Bonds	9.8%	13.2%	13.1%

bond holders receive the price promised at the bond's maturity and interest payments are halted. This happens when interest rates decline and bond issuers have an opportunity to borrow money at lower rates.

Because bonds provide investors with a fixed stream of revenue, they're considered very safe—as long as the issuer is financially secure. Bonds are rated on a scale from AAA, which indicates the issuer has a very good balance sheet, to D, which indicates that the bond is virtually worthless. Ratings of C and F, the lowest, also exist, but they are reserved for special cases. Bonds that are rated BB and B are considered junk bonds; they're usually bought as speculative investments. U.S. government bonds—also called Treasury bonds, Treasury notes, and Treasury bills, or T-Bills—are always rated AAA; municipal bonds may be rated much lower.

You'll find some variation in the performance of a bond mutual fund for the following reason: When interest rates in the general market fall below the rate that a particular bond is paying, the bond's value rises and the original bondholder can make a profit by selling the bond. When interest rates fall, the value of a bond drops and so will the shares of a bond mutual fund.

When you own a stock or equity fund you own a piece of a company. As a part owner, you may receive a share of the profits, known as a dividend, if the company chooses to issue one (many don't). Mutual funds that concentrate on dividend paying stocks have a steady stream of revenue, which helps make them more stable. The value of any stock is based on how the company is perceived by the rest of the world; if other people want to buy a piece, the price of stock goes up. If the company you're investing in isn't well thought of, investors who want to sell their shares have to take what the market will offer and the price drops.

On a typical day, a little more than half of all stocks in the various markets will rise while the others drop. There's a good reason most stocks tend to rise: The stock exchanges closely examine the business practices and records of the companies offering the stock and refuse to trade in stocks from companies that are in poor financial shape. Trading is halted in companies that suffer serious financial problems. A mutual fund can help the average investor avoid losing money on such sinking ships because mutual fund managers also inspect the books of companies they invest in and they'll be among the first to unload the stock of a troubled company. Small investors, who don't have the staff of a large mutual fund company, are likely to be the last to know about the daily status of their stock.

The risk in owning a stock mutual fund is that the fund will fall victim to a general market downturn or crash, when virtually all stocks in the market drop. Periodically, all funds drop in value but most rise again and go on to deliver profits to investors who held on to their shares through the down cycle. Only those who sold their shares when the fund was down lose money. For these reasons, it's important to plan your savings so you don't have all of your cash in a single mutual fund. You always want to keep some of your savings in a bank account, money market fund, or one of the most conservative bond funds to get you through emergencies.

Stock funds carry varying levels of risk depending on the types of companies they are invested in. Conservative stock funds are invested in only very large companies (sometimes called "blue chips") and aggressive growth stock funds look for smaller companies with good prospects.

Mutual Fund Vocabulary

- ➡ **Net asset value** The price of a share in a mutual fund, which is derived from the market value of the fund's holdings divided by the number of shares that have been issued.

- ➡ **No-load fund** Sells shares at the net asset value, with no additional fees.

- ➡ **Front-end load fund** A commission is charged on the price of each share purchased.

- ➡ **Exchange fee** Small charge incurred when you sell shares in one fund and buy a different fund offered by the same company.

- ➡ **Total fund operating expenses** The cost of managing the fund, which the fund managers deduct from the net asset value.

When you invest in either a stock or bond mutual fund, the amount you invest is converted to shares. For example, if you invested $1,000 in a fund on May 1 that was trading at $20 a share, you'd own 50 shares. Two months later, the value of the fund's assets may have risen to $21 a share. Your 50 shares would then be worth $1,050.

Mutual funds are profitable because the share price tends to rise over time, but funds also generate periodic payments. Each fund has its own schedule of either quarterly or annual disbursements. There are two basic forms of payment: capital gains, which are the profits the fund made by trading in stocks, and dividends. The mutual funds that generate the most consistent payments are bond funds and stock funds that invest in large companies that tend to pay dividends. Stock funds that invest in small companies and other speculative stocks are erratic; the capital gains distributions you receive are completely dependent on the fund's success in trading.

Unless you're planning to live off your investments, you'll want to reinvest capital gains and dividends. By doing so, you'll benefit from the technique of dollar cost averaging, which allows you to spread out your exposure to risk. In this case, your payments will be made as shares, which you'll buy at both low and high prices.

Choosing a Fund Strategy

Every healthy portfolio will have some built-in diversification. There's no magic formula, but you should aim for a mix that spreads your investment among high-risk and low-risk funds. You may wish to have your money invested for many years, but you should be prepared to tap into at least one of your funds for major purchases.

One way to control how much of a risk you're taking is to choose your funds carefully. Mutual funds can be classified into low-, moderate-, and high-risk funds. Government bond funds present the lowest risk, a mixture of bonds and stocks provide moderate risk, and growth stocks typically involve the highest risk. The general goal is to keep your investment in a high-risk fund as long as you won't need it. If you have a short-term goal (like saving up to buy a home), you will want most of your investments in lower-risk funds, with only a small amount—the part that will remain invested after you make the down payment—in higher-risk funds. If you have a long-term goal of more than five years (such as a college fund or retirement planning), you'll want to initially invest everything in higher-risk funds. Then you should move the money into moderate-risk funds gradually, and finally into lower-risk funds as the day you'll need the money grows near.

A mutual fund strategy should be based on planning for the years ahead. If you think you'll need some of the money that you've invested in a fund, start redeeming some of your shares in high-risk stock funds and investing the money in a moderate-risk fund one or two years ahead of time. Beginning about six months before you need the money, move your investment from the moderate-risk fund to a low-risk fund. This technique spreads out your risk because some of the shares will be redeemed at a higher value than others. This same principle of dollar-cost averaging applies to investing, too.

The average investor doesn't have just one goal for saving money. You may be saving for retirement, but you also need to keep assets liquid for new car purchases, vacations, and home maintenance. The consensus among financial experts is that several funds are needed to provide some measure of diversification, but it's rare for anyone to need more than six. By owning too many funds, you're likely to own the same stocks and bonds in different funds, and you end up wasting money on excessive management costs. The average stock fund company charged 1.55 percent in 1989, according to *Forbes Magazine*; the average bond fund company charged 1.08 percent. It's easy to forget about those costs because fund companies don't make a point of calling them to your attention. However, you can find them in your fund prospectus or in some of the performance reports available through online services.

Evaluating Mutual Fund Risk

Investment Objective	Level of Risk	Principle Investments
Money market	Low	CDs, Treasury bills
Short-term bond	Low	Government and corporate bonds of less than five-year maturities
Long-term bond	Moderate	Government and corporate bonds of 10 to 30 year maturities
Income	Moderate	Bonds and dividend paying stocks

Evaluating Mutual Fund Risk (Continued)

Investment Objective	Level of Risk	Principle Investments
Growth and Income	Moderate	Stocks that pay dividends and have growth potential
Convertible	Moderate	Preferred stocks and bonds that are convertible to common stock
International equity	High	Stocks of foreign companies
Sector	High	Stocks in a single industry, such as banking
Small company	High	Stocks in small companies with growth potential

Shopping for Mutual Funds Online

There are over 4,000 mutual funds vying for your attention. Some of them advertise, others are sold only by authorized financial planners or financial institutions. Some people choose funds based on the recommendations in magazine articles, other people rely on word-of-mouth. Comparing fund performance is not easy because they don't move in lockstep. In fact, if you compared two different funds over a ten-year period, there would be a big difference in which one performed better depending on when that ten-year period began. The only way to make a fair comparison is to look at a database that provides the same information on all funds. Advertisements that herald a fund as a leader in a specified period should be taken with a grain of salt.

➡ Finding a Fund by Its Ticker Symbols

One of the smartest ways to shop for a fund is to take advantage of the online services that have the data you really need. These services provide you with information about how well a mutual fund performed in the past and how it compares to other funds.

→ Finding a Fund by Its Ticker Symbols

Once you have an online account set up, the next thing you'll need to research mutual funds is the ticker symbol for the funds you want to investigate. These symbols resemble abbreviations for the fund name but many are far from obvious. For example, the symbol for Fidelity Investments Contrafund is FCNTX.

The symbols are official designations made by the stock exchanges and once you know a symbol, it's a good idea to record it somewhere because you'll need it anytime you want to get data about any type of a fund. (In Quicken, you can record it in your investment account.) Here's where you find ticker symbols on each of the services:

America Online	Use the Keyword Quote
CompuServe	Type Go Lookup
Prodigy	Use the Jumpword Quote

Choosing a fund by category is also difficult because the names themselves can be misleading. A fund that uses the words "capital appreciation" in its title could be either a high-risk aggressive growth fund or a moderate-risk balanced fund. You can do the research yourself by reading the *Wall Street Journal* day in and day out, or you can call an online service and use the databases there to pick the best fund for you in one sitting.

A mutual fund purchase is such an important investment, it's probably worthwhile to temporarily subscribe to one of these services simply for mutual fund shopping alone. The initial cost for subscribing to any of the these services will be less than $20—books that report mutual fund performance cost about twice that. The ongoing charges are based on monthly access plus surcharges for premium services, so if you want to plan a mutual fund research session, you should be able to get everything you need for less than $20, and then cancel the service without spending any more. (Both CompuServe and Prodigy classify their mutual fund databases as premium services; America Online has no surcharge.) In fact, you'll be able to do it free if you come across one of the introductory offers that provide a month's access time for free. These offers are often included in the box with new computers and modems.

Of the three services, America Online's mutual fund research service is the easiest to use. It's based on the work of Morningstar, a well respected mutual fund newsletter publisher. The emphasis is on finding the top performers by investment objective, which is Morningstar's specialty. Once you've logged onto America Online, find this section by selecting the keyword mutual fund. You'll then see a list of investment objectives. Select your preference from the list to see details on the top performing funds.

You can also get a historical performance report for any mutual fund that compares the fund to Standard & Poor's 500 index in recent years. Once you have the report displayed on your screen, select the Download option on America Online's File menu to save a copy on your computer. The reports are easy to read but they're not very detailed. If you use America Online often, you may want to take advantage of the Portfolio feature. This feature lets you record information about funds on your own, and every time you check here, you'll get an updated report on your current holdings.

Prodigy provides a more detailed level of reporting on each fund's performance. But it comes with a price: you have to pay a fee of about $6 to use it for a day. Prodigy's service is called The Mutual Fund Analyst, which is a data bank with detailed historical records on 3,400 funds. To find it, type the jumpword Mutual Fund Analyst. Once you've reached it, you'll see a menu that lets you choose the types of funds you're interested in researching by investment objective. You can also choose to limit the selection to a single company. For example, you may be happy with the Franklin Group and in searching for an aggressive growth fund, you'd want to be sure you investigated Franklin's offering. Here's how you could request reports on all mutual funds that the Franklin Group manages with the objective of aggressive growth: Choose Franklin Group from the Fund/Family Group option and then select Aggressive Growth from the Investment Objective option.

Once you've selected the report, the software will give you a choice of downloading the reports in either spreadsheet format (WK1, which all spreadsheets, including Microsoft Works, can read) or a delimited format, which is used to import data into databases. If you want to compare several funds, download each of them into spreadsheets, and then merge the individual files into one file. If you're using Microsoft Works to do this, first open a downloaded spreadsheet file, then, open another one of the downloaded files. Highlight the rows in that spreadsheet by clicking on the row numbers with your mouse. Then, select Cut on the Edit menu. Next, switch to the other spreadsheet by opening the Window menu and selecting the name. Once that spreadsheet is open, you can insert the data by first positioning your cursor on the cell where the new data should begin (probably a cell in column A) and then select Paste on the Edit menu. Repeat the process for each file you've downloaded.

Online Sources for Mutual Fund Facts

Service	How to Access	Description
America Online	Keyword: MUTUAL FUND	Morningstar ranking of top funds by category; historical performance of individual funds; tracks performance of your own portfolio
Prodigy	Jump: MUTUAL FUND ANALYST	Mutual Fund Analyst provides extensive historical data on individual funds
CompuServe	GO FUNDWATCH	Create rankings of funds by choosing the category you could consider most important: level of risk, investment objective, return by period, or fees. Also, reports on individual funds including current holdings.

On CompuServe, you'll find the best of what the other two services offer: fund rankings and detailed historical performance. Plus, you can do something not possible on the other services: you can generate your own list of the top-performing funds based on your own objectives. To reach CompuServe's mutual fund tools, type GO FUNDWATCH from any CompuServe prompt. You'll have a choice of finding the historical report on a particular fund or creating a ranking of the top performing funds. If you're shopping for funds, choose the option to screen top performing funds; after you create a ranking in the category of your choice, you can select funds you want to explore. The software will display the historical report for each so you can save it to your computer or print it out.

 ## Ranking funds with CompuServe's Money Watch

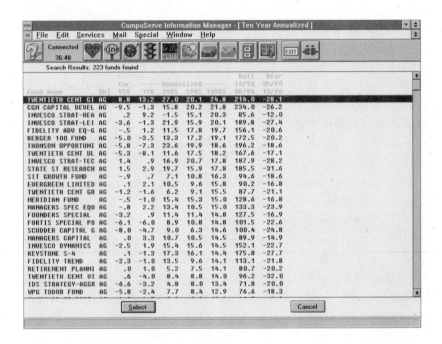

For example, let's say you were shopping for an aggressive, risk-taking fund that you planned to hold for a long time. When you reach the Money Watch opening screen, select Screen Top-Performing Funds. You will have a choice of eight different criteria; select Investment Objective. You'll then have nine choices, covering the basic mutual fund objectives. Select Aggressive Growth. The software will identify all of the funds it tracks in that category, displaying the number at the top of the screen. If it looks like the right number of funds, you can choose to display the funds by name. If it's a very large number, you may want to narrow the search to find a more manageable number of funds. Return to the main menu so you can customize the report some more if you wish. Perhaps you want to find only no-load funds. Select Loads and Fees, then select No-Load. The software will eliminate all of the funds that charge fees. You can continue to refine your selection further or just display the funds that meet your criteria. Before you can see the display of funds, you'll be asked to choose criteria for ranking the funds. Because we were looking for a long-term investment, Ten Year Annualized is the best choice. The software will next display all of the aggressive growth funds that don't charge load fees, ranked by their performance over the last ten years.

To continue your research, you'll want to find out more about some of the individual funds. If you're using CompuServe's own software CIM (CompuServe Information Manager), you can just double-click on the fund and a report will open. This report will include more detailed historical performance and a summary of the fund's current holdings. If you print the display that shows the ranking of all funds, and then the individual reports for every fund that you call up later, you'll have plenty of information for comparing the funds.

The report has some very valuable figures, such as how a specific fund performed compared to all other aggressive growth funds, and further compared with the overall Standard & Poor's (S&P's) index of stocks. Because you'll be gathering these reports on very similar funds, you can make some direct comparisons. If you want to get very technical, compare the beta coefficients of two different funds. This number indicates how volatile the fund has been. It's created by comparing the fund's price fluctuations with the fluctuations of the S&P 500. The S&P is considered to have a beta of 1.0; if a fund fluctuates 10 percent less than the S&P, it has a low beta of .9. A fund that fluctuates 10 percent more than the S&P has a beta of 1.1. High-risk funds will have high beta coefficients; low-risk funds will have low beta coefficients. Keep this in mind as you watch changes in the fund's share price in the future; you can take some comfort in knowing that those steep declines aren't a problem, they're supposed to happen.

You can also compare alpha ratings but if you've already ranked funds, you'll find that the ratings are similar. The alpha rating evaluates how well the fund has done compared with other funds in its investment objective. An alpha rating of 10 indicates the fund is in the top 10 percent of funds with similar objectives; a rating of 1.0 means the fund is in the bottom 10 percent of its class. Try to explore all of Money Watch; even the glossary is educational. While you can use it

FundWatch's Detailed Mutual Fund Report

Fund name

Investment objective

Level of volatility

How the fund did during good and bad periods

Total return to investors

How the fund compares to the Standard & Poor's Index

Stocks owned by the fund

```
                    TWENTIETH CENT GIFTRUST
                    INVESTORS RESEARCH CORP.
                          800-345-2021
                        Symbol: TWGTX

----------Assets & Yields---------    --------Expenses & Risk---------
Obj:                Aggressive Growth  Maximum Load Fee (%):          .00
Total Assets (Mil$):             184   Annual Expense Rate (%):       N/A
Net Asset Value Per Share:     19.08   Redemption Fee:                NO
Asset Allocation - % Cash:       6.0   12b-1 Fee:                     NO
Asset Allocation - % Fixed:       .0   Beta Coefficient:            1.384
Asset Allocation - % Equity:    94.0   Alpha Rating (10-1):           1
Latest 12-Mo Divd Yield (%):     .00   Risk Rating (10-1):           10
SEC482 % Yield - 06/30/94:       N/A   Diversified vs. S&P 500 (%):  40
----------------------Performance Ratings----------------------
Overall Rating (10-1):        5      Rating in AG Group (10-1):       8

----------------------Relative Performance----------------------
                                                          Bull   Bear
                  Curr   Curr --------Annualized-------- 10/90  5/90
As of  9/30/94   Month   YTD   1YR  3YRS  5YRS  10YRS   8/94  10/90
-----------------------------------------------------------------
Fund % Return     8.16   8.84 13.28 27.07 20.14 24.81  214.0  -28.1
Avg. AG Fund       -.6  -1.7   -.3  10.1  10.5  13.1  105.7  -22.2
S&P 500           -2.5   1.3   3.7   9.1   9.1  14.6   75.3  -14.5
AG Group Rank       10    10    10    10    10    10     10      3
Overall Rank        10    10    10    10    10    10     10      1
---Portfolio By Sector(%)---   -----------Top Stock Holdings----------
                          S&P                          Mkt Value   %
Sector              Fund  500  Stock Name                ($000)  Port
-----------------   ----  ---  --------------------    --------- ----
Basic Industries      9    8   MICROCHIP TECHNOLOGY IN   14,276   8.5
Cap Goods & Tech     39   15   ENERGY SVC INC            11,812   7.0
Consumer Cyclical    20   16   FASTENAL CO                5,062   3.0
Consumer Stable      15   20   COMMUNITY HEALTH SYS IN    4,770   2.8
Energy                9   10   IDEXX LABORATORIES CORP    4,611   2.7
Finance               3   12   MICROS SYS INC             4,372   2.6
Transportation        2    2   SEITEL INC                 4,256   2.5
Utilities             0   14   NORAND CORP                4,200   2.5
Miscellaneous         4    4   CERNER CORP                4,079   2.4
                               STATESMAN GROUP INC        4,043   2.4

--Weighted Avg. P/E Ratio---   ------Weighted Average Cap. (Bil$)------
TWENTIETH CENT GIFTRUST 27.0   TWENTIETH CENT GIFTRUST               .4
S&P 500                 21.0   S&P 500                             20.3
```

to help you buy funds, you should periodically check in here to see how your current holdings compare with the rest of the market.

Keeping Track of Your Funds

For years, mutual fund investors who wanted to see how their holdings were doing had to rely on printed statements that the fund companies mailed either annually or quarterly. If they wanted an update, they could squint over the financial pages of a newspaper to find the fund listing and then calculate the value of their holdings by multiplying the latest price by the number of shares held when the last statement was printed.

 ### Tracking Mutual Funds in a Quicken Investment Account

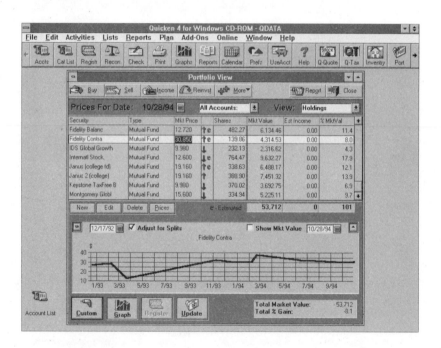

Now, you can use Quicken to store the mutual fund data in a register and automatically update the price by pressing a button. Quicken will dial a phone number, connect your computer modem with a quote service, and insert the new price directly into your Quicken register. To take advantage of this service, you need to have recorded the amount of your holdings for each mutual fund in an investment register and you need to have entered the correct ticker symbol for each fund. Then, select Online from the Quicken main menu and choose Update Portfolio Prices. The program will automatically dial a local phone number and insert the new prices in the Portfolio view. (Quicken attempts to dial a local number first but if one is not available in your area, it will use an 800 number instead.) You can use the service three times for free; after that, the software will set up an account that automatically bills your credit card for using the service. The updated prices can be seen only by opening the Portfolio view (select it on the Activities menu). With the Portfolio view open, be sure to select the Graphs function; it will give you an overview of your mutual fund growth. You will notice that the software does not change prices in your register; that's because you have not recorded a new transaction.

If you don't want to use Quicken, or you want to perform a more detailed analysis of your holdings than Quicken provides, you'll want to create your own spreadsheet to record information. The easiest way to set up a mutual fund spreadsheet is to follow the layout of your mutual fund statement. Every company has its own design for reporting results and it will be easiest if you name the columns in your spreadsheet according to categories on the statement.

A typical mutual fund statement starts with the date in the left column and so that's how the spreadsheet shown on the next page starts. The first date records when the fund was opened although if you're keeping track of an existing fund, you can use the current date. The following categories can be in any order you like but you'll enter figures in all cells only for the very first entries. From then on, there are only three cells where you will enter a specific figure: the date, the price of a share, and the number of shares earned. Every other cell should be calculated with a formula, including how much your current holdings are worth, how many shares you own, and how much you earned on a specific statement.

To build your own spreadsheet, refer to the same screen shown on this page. (This spreadsheet is not included on the book's companion CD-ROM because the reports from mutual funds vary so much, it would be impossible to provide a spreadsheet matching every reader's needs.) In the top part of the screen, you

Do-It-Yourself: A Mutual Fund Tracker

Formula that calculates monthly dividend

Formula that calculates total shares

Formula that calculates dollars held

see how the spreadsheet looks during normal use. The bottom of this screen shows what has been entered into each cell: Some cells contain numbers, others display formulas. The very first row of data will be prices and numbers of shares based on the actual purchase of shares. In the second row, you start to enter formulas. Once you've entered the first row correctly, you can copy the formulas to the following rows, by selecting the row, cutting it, and then pasting it into the following row. The spreadsheet will automatically adjust the formulas to use the correct cell references.

The cell that calculates the amount on the statement shown (monthly dividend in a bond fund) multiples the share price times the number of shares earned on this statement (in this sample, the formula is =C7*D7, which shows that in row 7 the monthly dividend was calculated by multiplying the contents of cell C7 by D7. To calculate total shares, you need to add the shares being reported on this statement to the shares held as of the last statement (=D7+E6). And to calculate the total value of your account, you need to multiply the current number of shares times the current price (=C7*E7).

Once you've recorded a few months worth of data, you'll want to graph the performance of the spreadsheet to show how the total number of dollars has grown. Try it sometime when you're feeling discouraged about your financial picture. It just may cheer you up.

5 | *Investing: Stocks*

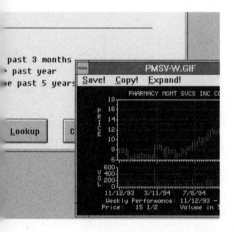

76 What Online Services Can—
and Can't—Do

78 How to Research Stocks with
Dow Jones

80 Researching Stocks with
CompuServe

85 How to Research Stocks with
Prodigy

88 How to Research Stocks on
the Internet

90 Trading with Online Brokers

To make money in the stock market, you must have two things: access to information and ability to use that information. While it takes years of practice and hard work to develop the ability to trade stocks successfully, you can gain access to the information you'll need almost instantly with your home computer. This information will be of use to you regardless of the course you take in your investing. If you want to invest on your own, your computer provides the basic tools. If you decide to work with a stock market professional, you'll still benefit from being more informed, and you can begin building the knowledge you'll need to become a successful stock-picker.

To get started, all that's required is your computer and an online service. This chapter will show you how to do the following:

✔ Research stocks with Dow Jones

✔ Research stocks with CompuServe

✔ Research stocks with Prodigy

✔ Research stocks on the Internet

✔ Trade using online brokers

But first, a little background.

What Online Services Can—and Can't—Do

Online services provide exhaustive data banks full of company reports, financial forecasts, and historical stock prices, and they offer access to online stock trading services.

However, while small investors can find online all the basic tools needed to start trading, they're still at a disadvantage compared to the professional stock trader. This is because business information—and knowledge—do not come cheap. For example, all online stock trading services are similar to discount brokers: They are inexpensive, but they do not provide advice, they merely execute trade orders. A full-service broker charges far more for each trade than a trading service because the broker's real service is advice on when to buy which stocks, and when to sell. A full-service broker will help an investor build a portfolio specially designed for his or her needs: full of aggressive picks at some times and balanced with safer choices at others. Most important, a full-service broker is steeped in knowledge of market trends. You can only know how to time trades if you're paying close attention to market trends, reading the very latest financial forecasts, and have the ability to analyze what you've discovered.

A typical small investor will spend an hour or two a week researching stocks, at a cost of about $25 a month in online connect charges; professional traders pay thousands of dollars a month for access to the best information, and they monitor it constantly every business day. As an individual, you can't afford to spend that much to buy information, and you don't have the time to review business reports throughout the day. And you probably haven't had years of experience.

That's why, even with a personal computer at home, many investors still prefer to use the services of a full-service stock broker, who will monitor the market, proffer advice, and execute trades. These investors use their personal computer to keep track of their investments and follow general market trends, but they recognize stock trading to be a specialized skill that is worth the extra money full-service brokers charge.

If you choose to start investing on your own, start with just a small amount (less than 10 percent of your savings), carve out time to research the stocks you buy, and then continue to research them for as long as you own shares. There's no guarantee you'll make money at first, but if you keep working at it, you're likely to succeed in the long run. If you already have experience with basic stock analysis, then all you need to do is become familiar with the wealth of data you'll find available through online services.

A Stock Picker's To-Do List	Online Services to Use
1. Spot hot stocks	Vestor and S&P on CompuServe Wall St. Edge and Stock Hunter on Prodigy Innovest on Dow Jones
2. View price history	Company Analyzer on CompuServe Tradeline on Prodigy Tradeline on Dow Jones

A Stock Picker's To-Do List	Online Services to Use
3. Read balance sheet	Company Analyzer on CompuServe Strategic Investor on Prodigy Dun's reports on Dow Jones
4. Search for recent news	Company Analyzer on CompuServe Company News on Prodigy *Wall Street Journal* archives on Dow Jones

How to Research Stocks with Dow Jones

You can find at least a little financial information on just about any online service, but the undisputed leader is the Dow Jones News/Retrieval Service. It's run by the same company that publishes the *Wall Street Journal* and is so well-respected in the financial community that the company's device for taking a pulse of the market—the Dow Jones Averages—is the most widely quoted measure of the stock market. Here you'll find thorough reports on all American corporations and exhaustive analyses of stock prices over the years. But the best costs the most. The Dow Jones News/Retrieval Service charges $1.50 per 1,000 characters displayed, with higher fees for special reports; you can easily spend over $100 an hour as you explore the menu choices.

Fortunately, Dow Jones offers a special deal. Dow Jones Market Monitor lets you access much of the same information for about $30 a month if you're willing to call between the hours of 7 p.m. and 6 a.m. on weekdays or any time over the weekend. You can't use some of the most exclusive features—such as Dunn & Bradstreet's detailed corporate reports that cost about $100 through the main Dow Jones service—but you can download data that are invaluable to an investor.

For example, you can search through over 90,000 reports filed by economists and Wall Street analysts. The reports are compiled by Thomson Financial Services and provide opinions on the prospects for industries and individual companies. These reports are the basis for many stock brokers' buy-and-sell recommendations.

➔ *Save Money by Saving Files*

Research using online services can be expensive because you're usually paying by the minute. But you can keep your bill down by saving first and reading later. Save reports to your hard disk whenever you find data that look promising. After you've disconnected from the online service, you can read the report and print hard copy at your leisure.

Saving reports on stocks and companies requires that you learn how to use your program's File Save options. Capturing a text report is not the same as downloading a file. When you download a file, you can't read the file before you start the download process, and there's a specific procedure that's originated by the online service. When you capture a text file, you won't get any prompting from the remote service and you won't use the download command. Usually, you turn on the File-Save option in your communications software, and every piece of text that is displayed by the online service will be captured to a file on your computer. Different communications programs have different terms for this command. In ProComm Plus it's called Capture File, in Windows Terminal it's called Receive Text File, and in CompuServe CIM it's called File-Save.

The easiest way to save everything is to turn on the capture process as soon as you start doing your research. You'll end up with a very large file that you'll have to sort through later but you won't miss anything valuable. If you are certain you want only a specific report, start the capture process just before you're about to tell the online service to display the file, and then end the capture as soon as the report is completely displayed. In most cases, the reports you want to read are displayed by online services one screen at a time, so you have an opportunity to see a little bit before you decide if it's worth keeping.

Innovest Technical Analysis provides opinions on a stock's near-term prospects after computing an analysis of market conditions that covers over 25,000 variables. All you do is enter the stock symbol and you receive a clear opinion. You'll be told whether the stock is likely to rise or drop and the stock's likely price range for the next 50 days. Innovest recommendations have to be taken in context because its technical analysis looks only at a stock's price in relation to the entire market and doesn't consider business conditions. Thus, while a company with great technical analysis indicators might be about to nosedive because of a lawsuit or a collapse in its product sales, Innovest's recommendation wouldn't take this situation into account.

But you can also check the news for reports on individual companies. Market Monitor lets you view any article that appeared in the *Wall Street Journal* in the past 10 years and in *Barron's* and *Business Week* since 1985. However, Market Monitor is difficult to use. It's easy to get lost because you must memorize menu commands and often need to enter a slash for some instructions or two slashes for others.

For the average investor, the most practical choices for financial research are CompuServe and Prodigy. They're much easier to use, and they have some of the information that's available on the Dow Jones services—for example, distilled versions of the reports available on Dow Jones, tailored to the individual investor. If you already have a subscription to either service, don't switch until you've exhausted all that it has to offer. But if you are planning to start using an online service just for managing your stock investments, the following pages will help you decide. You may decide you'll need both CompuServe and Prodigy to have all of the features you need. Subscribing to two services isn't as expensive as you may think. Remember that the basic subscription cost of each is low at about $10, but the real cost of using the service can be three or four times that much when you use extended or premium services. As we look at some of the tools you can use to research stocks, you'll find that while both CompuServe and Prodigy have the essential databases, each has some unique services that you may find invaluable in managing your portfolio.

Researching Stocks with CompuServe

CompuServe is a serious place. It's run by H & R Block, the tax-return people, and there's a no-nonsense approach to distributing information that appeals to busy people. CompuServe doesn't have a lot of educational tools for learning about investing, but it does give you access to financial information that is designed for the small investor.

➡ CompuServe's Money Menu

The best place to begin researching a stock is the Money menu (type go money from any CompuServe ! prompt) where you see a list of all of CompuServe's investment aids. The first few items are Basics Services, which means you pay only the CompuServe connect time and no extra fees. Your first research tool is the Basic Quote option. You'll find the current price for any stock, trading volume (the number of shares that have changed hands so far that day), most recent price bid, and most recent price asked. To see the quote, you need to type in the stock's ticker symbol. If you don't know the ticker symbol for a stock, you can use Issue Symbol/Lookup on the Money menu (it's also a Basic service). Be sure to write down all of the symbols you request. You'll use them over and over in your research.

With an idea of a stock's trading price, you'll be ready to learn something about the company. On CompuServe, your least expensive option is the Hoover Company Database, which is part of the Basic Service plan. The Hoover databases are designed for the average investor who wants a synopsis of a company in plain language. The reports are broken into topics that answer the "who, what, when, and where" of a company's structure. Most important is the How Much topic, which displays a balance sheet for the past five years. You'll find a company's earnings reports and analysis of the share price, including fluctuations in the stock's annual price-to-earnings ratio. The Hoover Company Database is a good place to start learning about companies, but savvy investors will find it much too general and out of date. For example, the financial reports offered can be over a year old.

That's about all you can do to research stocks without spending extra. To find information of greater depth on CompuServe, you need to pay for some of the Extended Services. All are listed on the same Money menu, just below the Basic Services. For example, you may want a closer look at a stock price than just today's quote; on the Extended Services menu you can select Historical Stock/Fund Pricing

➡ Reading a balance sheet on CompuServe

Reports in the Hoover Company Databases detail a corporation's financial results in recent years.

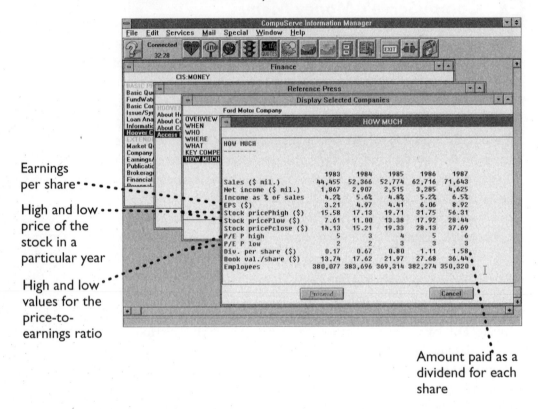

Earnings per share••••

High and low price of the stock in a particular year

High and low values for the price-to-earnings ratio

Amount paid as a dividend for each share

and find the prices for a stock over the past five years. If you choose Price Volume Graph and you're using CompuServe's CIM, you can see a chart showing how the price has changed combined with the volume of trading in the stock. The extra cost isn't significant. Most of these displays are a dollar or less.

Before you invest in a company, you really should know more about it than the cursory information that Hoover Company Database supplies. CompuServe's research database includes a variety of specialized services such as credit reports and SEC filings, but for the average investor, one of the best ways to learn all you can about a stock is by using CompuServe's Company Analyzer service. Select it

➡️ *Charting a stock's history*

CompuServe's extended services let you view the fluctuations in a stock price as a chart.

Ticker symbol for a stock

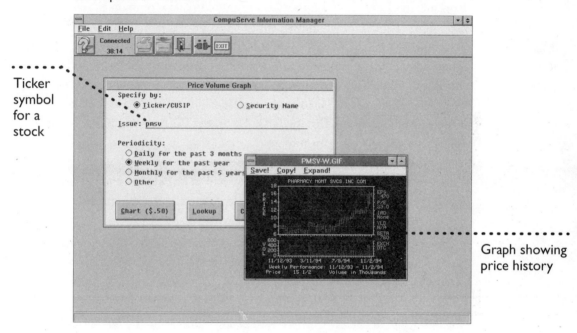

Graph showing price history

from the Money menu and you'll find a summary of the best research available on CompuServe for evaluating a company's prospects. You can find balance sheets, cash flow reports, and quarterly income statements that are updated frequently. There are also statements from company officials and a wealth of detail (including salaries for senior officials). There's even a summary of recent news reports about the company. The Company Analyzer menu is a collection of reports, most of which require a separate fee. Some of the fees are as little as fifty cents; others are $10 each. You'll spend about $20 if you use all of the choices, so you won't want to use it often, but you should consider using it before you buy stock in a company.

If you're close to a buying a stock, your next step should be InvesText on CompuServe. It provides a combination of financial analysis and professional

⊝ The Best Way to Navigate CompuServe

CompuServe can be used with any personal communications software program, including ProComm, SmartComm, and Delrina Communications Suite. But you'll save time and get more from the service if you use the software on this book's CD-ROM. (Just click on the Your Online Connection to CompuServe button for more information.) CompuServe Information Manager (CIM) completely manages your connection to CompuServe, providing menu selections that can help guide you through the service and make downloading files easier. CompuServe Navigator (CSNav) is software that will retrieve information from many CompuServe areas quickly so you can reduce the amount of time you're connected to the service. You give the software instructions on the type of information to retrieve and the software dials the modem, downloads the information, and then lets you browse through it at your leisure.

While you can retrieve some financial reports and participate in financial discussion areas, you can't trade or play stock-trading games with Navigator.

You can transfer either program from CompuServe's computers to your own by following menu choices. To find the command that will begin the transfer, type GO CISSOFT at any CompuServe prompt and follow the menu choices. If you use CompuServe often, you'll want both programs. Use CIM to explore CompuServe and use CSNav when you know what you want.

opinion and appears as a choice on the U.S. Company Information menu. (You can reach it directly by typing "go investext" at any CompuServe prompt). This service carries hefty fees of about $20 per report, but the information may prove so valuable you'll consider it a bargain. InvesText compiles reports from brokerage house analysts, and they're comparable to the information that a professional stock broker receives. You'll find clear opinions on whether a stock is worth buying, projections about the company's finances, and data to support the positions. If you're not using a full-service stock broker, you owe it to yourself to consider this service before you invest in any stock. In addition to reports on companies, you'll also find reports on the outlook for specific industries.

Expert opinions on a stock's prospects

The InvesText service on CompuServe provides reports from Wall Street analysts, including opinions on the prospects for a company's stock.

How to Research Stocks with Prodigy

Prodigy is designed to be easy to use, and that philosophy is apparent throughout the service. For starters, you don't have a choice in software: You must use software supplied by Prodigy (it's available at most retail stores). And while Prodigy has some serious analytic tools for the investor, the information is usually presented graphically so you often see easy-to-read tables and charts, rather than the densely packed reports you'll find on CompuServe. The most significant difference between CompuServe and Prodigy is not the information but the style in which you find it. The reports you find on both services are supplied by financial publishers; in many cases, the information is basically the same—much of it from stock prices and balance sheets—but the presentations differ dramatically. Some people prefer Prodigy simply because it's more appealing to view, and much of the financial information is presented in a way that's easier to understand than on CompuServe.

➜ Prodigy's Tradeline

For example, when you look up a stock price using Prodigy's Tradeline service, you can see the information as a table, view it as a chart, or download the underlying information. On CompuServe, you can view charts for stock prices only if you're using CIM software. And you can download the prices only as they're displayed; you'll then have to edit the data—removing the extra text and line spaces that are part of the display—if you want to use the information in a spreadsheet. Prodigy lets you download the stock in several formats: Quicken data files, metastock, or comma-delimited format. If you use a spreadsheet, comma-delimited format will be easy to import; the spreadsheet recognizes the commas as cell separators. You find Prodigy's stock history information by using the jumpword tradeline or by selecting Price History from the Research menu in the Business and Finance section.

Prodigy's strength is in presenting stock price information. It provides less help than CompuServe in understanding a company. Most of Prodigy's reports are based on stock price fluctuations and news about companies. You won't find the kind of background information that CompuServe provides, such as annual reports or Securities and Exchange Commission filings, but you will find plenty of advice on where the market is going.

➡ **Prodigy makes it easy to view price charts**

Prodigy presents information from the Tradeline service in a graphical display that includes both stock price changes and comparisons to the Standard & Poor 500.

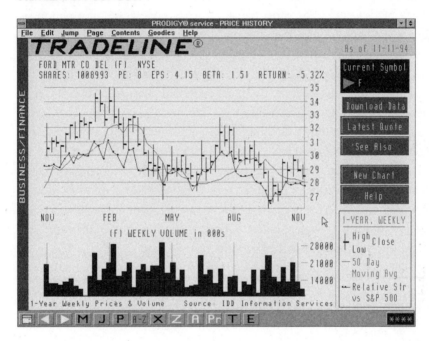

To learn about a company on Prodigy, you can search through reports from the Dow Jones News/Retrieval service, including articles in the *Wall Street Journal* and *Barron's*. These articles are presented under the banner of Company News, and they can be searched by a company's name. For financial analysis of a company, Prodigy provides Strategic Investor, a report that consists of financial reports based mainly on the relationship between a company's earnings and its stock price. Strategic Investor costs $15 a month in addition to Prodigy connect charges. You can find either service by using the service name as a jumpword.

It's important to feel like an insider when you're trading stocks, no matter how far removed you are from Wall Street. Prodigy helps by giving you access to some of the newsletters that analyze current trends and make forecasts. In Prodigy's Wall

St. Edge you can read a digest of 13 financial newsletters, complete with stock picks and opinions on where the market is heading. Access to this section is sold for a fee of $2 a day. To find it, use the jumpword Wall St. Edge.

Finally, Prodigy delivers what is arguably the richest source of stock picks available to the public anywhere. The Stock Hunter service presents over 100 stock picks weekly. You must pay a fee of $6 to view the information for a day, but Stock Hunter delivers information that is clearly worth much more to serious investors. Stock Hunter applies some of the more popular stock-picking theories to real data. These theories can usually be boiled down to a formula: Find the stocks that display the most extreme behavior in several categories, and you'll have winners in the future.

A credible strategy usually requires a combination of careful research and cold analysis. First, you have to identify the stocks that have changed the most in a particular category, and then you have to apply the formula. In the past, to take advantage of one of these strategies, you would need to put in long hours, compiling results and calculating the strategic formula. Prodigy's Stock Hunter is a shortcut for the average investor. Each week, it crunches the number for the eight leading strategies and shows the results.

The eight strategies that Prodigy tracks include Peter Lynch's theory, which he detailed in his best-selling book, *One Up on the Street*. Other strategies include Graham/Dodd, which looks for securities that are 20% below their theoretical value as computed by the Graham/Dodd Adjusted P/E model, and Wallflowers, which attempts to identify small firms with good growth potential that have not yet attracted the attention of institutional investors. The theories are spelled out in detail when you view the service, so you can decide for yourself if this form of stock-picking is worth your time and money.

How to Research Stocks on the Internet

The Internet will make you work a little harder for your information, but if you're comfortable using Telnet and Gopher services on the Internet, you may be able to save money by doing some of your financial research this way.

Where to Find Hot Tips

Online Service	Directions	What You'll Find
CompuServe	go s&p	Two lists from Standard & Poors. A Master List of conservative choices and an Investment Ideas list of more speculative choices.
CompuServe	Go vestor	Both buy and sell advice based on applying a proprietary technical analysis program created by Asset Advisory Corp.
Prodigy	Jump: stock hunter	Results of applying eight different theories to market data.
Prodigy	Jump: wall st edge	A digest of newsletters reveals the picks of market analysts
Dow Jones	//GUIDE	Innovest Technical Analysis provides buy, sell, hold recommendations on all publicly traded stocks
America Online	Keyword: DP	Decision Point provides buy and sell recommendations on 150 volatile stocks; also tips are found in 13 newsletters from market analysts.

Edgar is an information server that distributes all reports filed with the SEC. These filings detail significant financial events at publicly traded companies, and they're closely followed by professional investors. The reports are difficult reading, but contain the hard data that stock analysts use in forming their opinions on a stock's prospects. On CompuServe, you pay about $10 for each report, but on the Internet, you will pay only for the connect time of your Internet service provider.

➔ *Internet Connecting*

To find the service, use your Internet software to search Gopherspace for "edgar." For basic stock-price information, including historical reports and P/E ratios, you can use QuoteCom. To access QuoteCom databases, use Telnet to reach "quote.com" or send e-mail to "services@quote.com." If you're using the World Wide Web, you can use a QuoteCom service to receive announcements that major companies post to a service called PR Newswire. To start using these reports, you'll need to connect to the QuoteCom web server by using this command http /www.quote.com/register/reg-prnews.html.

Trading with Online Brokers

After you've sifted through all of your tips, done your homework, and made your decision on what to buy, you may want to fall back on the traditional full-service broker rather than using one of the online brokers. The advantage of using a full-service broker is the reality check—you may think you've uncovered a gold mine, but your broker may be privy to information that you didn't uncover. A broker will also provide advice on creating a balanced portfolio. Maybe you didn't realize that all of your stocks are in cyclical industries; when the economy shifts, your portfolio will suffer.

On the other hand, maybe you prefer to do it yourself. You don't trust anyone to handle your money, and you don't want to be bothered with advice you don't need. Most important, you don't want to pay the rates of a full-service broker when a discount broker charges only about $25 and $50 per trade. If that's you, then using an online broker will be an improvement over using a discount broker by phone. Your online account can be viewed at any hour, showing the value of your current holdings and how it's changed over time.

Online brokers are available through the major online services, plus some have their own access numbers that aren't connected with the online services. For example, you can use the Charles Schwab Brokerage Service either through the GeNIE online service or by using the company's own software. Fidelity

➜ *Playing Before You Pay*

If you've never traded stocks online, don't learn by risking your own money. Take advantage of the simulated trading program offered by E*Trade on CompuServe and America Online. You can learn by playing. The stock simulator gives you $100,000 worth of play money and sets up an account that will last for a month. You can invest the money any way you please in either stocks or options. At the end of the month, the program declares a winner and awards a $50 prize.

Playing the simulated trade will let you try out some of your theories in stocks at the same time you become familiar with the software. To find the game, you can hunt through the Money menu's Brokerage choices, or type "go etgame" on CompuServe, or use the keyword "stocks on America Online. The software will guide you through the sign-up process. You'll receive a password to limit access to your account, and you'll view the rules of the game.

Finding Online Stock Brokers

Brokerage	Where to Find It	Parent Brokerage
TickerScreen on CompuServe	On CompuServe, type go tkr	Max Ule
E*Trade on CompuServe	On CompuServe, type go etrade	Trade Plus
QuikWay on CompuServe	On CompuServe, type go qwk	Quick & Reilly
TradePlus on America Online	Keyword: stocks	TradePlus
PCFN on Prodigy	Jumpword: PCFN	Donaldson, Lufkin & Jenrette

Investments also has its own trading software, FOX, but it's available only by connecting directly with Fidelity's own computers.

It makes sense to use an online broker that's offered by the same online service you frequent. You'll find it's easier to keep track of your investments if you have to make just one phone call, especially when you find the need to do some research on one of your investments. For example, let's say you've just checked your portfolio and found that one of your holdings has started dropping. The first thing you'll want to do is search through the latest news to learn if there's been a development that's caused the drop. If you're using a broker on an online service, you can leave your broker's software, search the news, and then immediately return to the broker's software to place a sell or buy order.

Trading stocks through online brokers is completely electronic except for one thing: you'll need to mail a check to open the account, and you'll receive a check in the mail when you close the account. To get started, you follow the menu choices displayed by the online service. Some online trading services will let you execute your first trade the day you sign up, pending receipt of a check from you. Other services wait until they've received your check before you can begin to trade.

To start trading, you'll enter a buy order. The software will give you the choice of buying at the current market rate or let you select a price, called the limit price. If you select a limit, the trade will not be executed until the stock reaches your price. Usually, limit prices have expiration periods, and if the stock doesn't hit your price within the time period, the order will automatically expire.

Once an order has been executed, the broker's software will keep a portfolio record showing the number of shares you own, the current price of shares, and how much your holding is worth. It will also show your "basis" (the amount you invested initially) and how much you've gained or lost since you bought the stock. Since the portfolio is in table form, you'll be able to download the information to your own computer and store the record in a spreadsheet. If you're tracking your stocks in Quicken, you can set up the purchase of the stock as a transaction in an Investment account. The only information you'll need to set up the Quicken account is the number of shares purchased, the price per share, and the amount of commission paid. Quicken will then be able to calculate the value of your investment even if you enter a new share price. If you want, you can have Quicken update the price automatically by selecting the Update Portfolio Price option on Quicken's Online menu. You can use the service three times for free, and then you'll pay about $1 a call. Most people will find it makes more sense to update the prices themselves in Quicken. If you're using an online broker, you get the information for normal connect charges, which will almost always work out to be dramatically less than Quicken's service.

Placing a buy order on Prodigy

The PC Financial Network is Prodigy's discount broker; trades are executed by the brokerage house Donaldson, Lufkin & Jenrette.

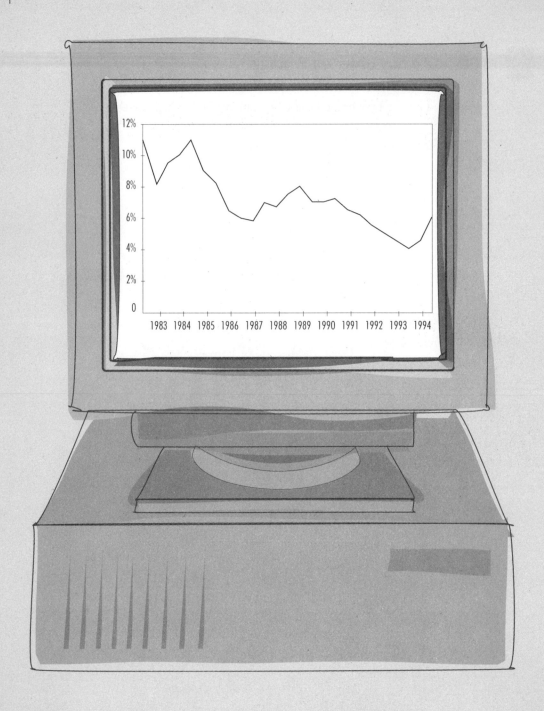

6 *Saving* at the Highest **Rates**

96 Finding the Best Savings Bank
Interest Rates

98 Calculating the Value of
Savings Bonds

All of us need a safe haven for some of our money. Your general outlook on life determines exactly how much of your savings becomes tied up in safe investments, but you should have between 10 and 25 percent in rock-solid instruments like federally insured savings bank accounts, and U.S. government savings bonds, where the returns are guaranteed and the principle is insured.

This type of security will give you peace of mind. And while these investments won't make you rich—their interest rates are historically several percentage points lower than mutual funds and stocks—all of them deliver higher returns than the interest in a typical checking account. If you shop wisely, you can gain an extra percentage point or two over the average interest rates on comparable accounts.

This chapter will show you how to do the following:

✔ Find the highest savings bank interest rates
✔ Calculate the value of savings bonds

First, we'll explore some online tools for finding the best rates on money market savings accounts and certificates of deposit (CDs). Then, on the companion CD-ROM, we'll look at the program, EEBond, which calculates the return on savings bonds.

Finding the Best Savings Bank Interest Rates

Bankers structure savings options according to a simple rule: The best interest rates go to accounts with the greatest restrictions. The lowest interest rates are found in the simple passbook accounts, sometimes called statement savings or just plain savings accounts, that have the fewest restrictions on when money can be withdrawn. If you have only a few hundred dollars, a bank savings account is probably the only safe avenue for building your savings, and you should take advantage of it. But your goal should be to amass enough to open a higher-yielding money-market savings account. Some banks are starting to place minimum deposit rules on savings accounts, so you may need to shop around to find a bank that offers a true passbook savings account.

Everyone with more than $1,000 will have little need for a passbook account. Money you may need on very short notice can be kept in an interest-bearing checking account, and money set aside for a rainy day should be kept in a money-market savings account at higher interest rates.

Money-market accounts have interest rates that change to reflect market conditions, but they're always significantly higher than passbook savings interest rates. Money-market accounts usually have only one restriction: a required minimum deposit of at least $500. These accounts are perfectly safe since they are protected by FDIC guarantee, which means the Federal Deposit Insurance Corporation will reimburse any depositors if the bank fails.

Finding the best rates for money-market accounts has been difficult. Most people rely on their local bank or are attracted by newspaper ads. If you wanted to embark on a real comparison of interest rates, you'd need to call banks by phone and inquire about rates and minimum deposit requirements.

➔ Money-Market Shopping with a Modem

Your computer can help you do a much better job at money-market shopping if you have a modem and an account with CompuServe. From any CompuServe prompt, type GO RATEGRAM and you'll find a menu offering reports for a variety of investments. You will be billed extra for using this service—about a dollar per report above normal CompuServe connect charges—but this information can help you earn several hundred dollars in extra interest.

The Rategram menu lists money market accounts as "Liquid Money Market Accounts ($)." The "liquid" description indicates that these accounts have no time limit: you can remove the money whenever you need it. The ($) indicates your CompuServe bill will be charged for reading this report. Another menu item details current surcharges but in recent years, the charges have been about one dollar per report.

→ Money-Market Shopping with a Modem

Before you open the report, make sure you know how to either print or save online information to your disk. You'll want to have a copy of the data to refer to after you sign off. Don't try to jot down the bank phone numbers with a pen while you're viewing the report—there's far too much information to write down. You'll want to go down the list after you've logged off CompuServe and call these banks for details. Some banks may have changed their rates or minimum deposit requirements already, so you may need to shop quite a bit before you find the right money-market account. The RateGram report includes bank phone numbers, addresses, current rates, and minimum deposit requirements.

If you're able to keep your money in one place for a longer period, you can earn higher interest rates with a CD (certificate of deposit). These bank accounts are also insured by the government and offer higher interest rates than money-market accounts. You can earn the highest CD rates by committing your money to longer periods of deposit, ranging from six months to five years.

You'll find a comparison of CD rates on the same Rategram menu where money-market accounts are listed. You can shop among CD rates by the length of the account term. Be sure to save these lists to a disk file or print them so you can comparison shop after you've disconnected from CompuServe.

Calculating the Value of Savings Bonds

Government savings bonds have been popular for decades because they're backed by the U.S. Treasury. They're popular as gifts, since the investment is represented by a single, beautifully engraved piece of paper entitling the bondholder to a fixed amount at the date of maturity, which will be honored at any commercial bank. And many people buy bonds with a savings bond payroll plan.

The return on savings bonds was fixed for decades, but in 1982, with interest rates rising, the government changed the interest rate from 4 percent to market-

Shopping for the best bank rates

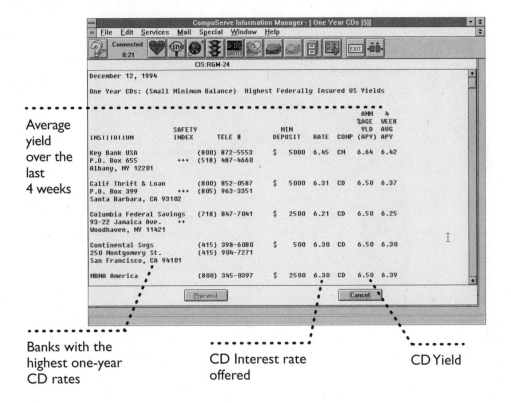

Average yield over the last 4 weeks

Banks with the highest one-year CD rates

CD Interest rate offered

CD Yield

based rate. The change in interest rates made the bonds more lucrative, but the earnings on a bond are now very difficult to calculate.

Series EE savings bonds now earn 85 percent of the average market yield on Treasury securities during the time the bond is held. The market yields are averages of the Treasury 5-year constant maturities, calculated daily and averaged monthly by the Department of the Treasury. Because a savings bond can continue to earn interest for years after it's earned the face value of the bond, you can only determine the exact value of a bond by working through a long string of numbers.

The return on U.S. savings bonds

The change to a market-based interest rate has made calculating the return on bonds difficult. Your computer can help. Here's how the rate has varied since 1983.

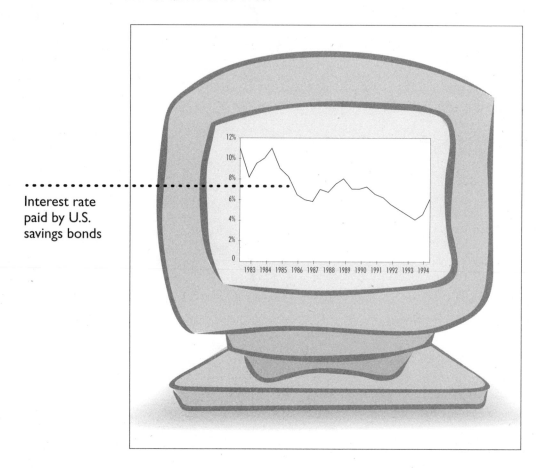

Interest rate paid by U.S. savings bonds

The Treasury Department's Bureau of Public Debt performs these calculations and then publishes a table establishing the rates paid on various bonds.

Not only do interest rates vary, but the interest-bearing life of bonds has changed over the years; some old bonds earned interest for 40 years, others have lives of 30 or 20 years. It's not unusual for people to hold bonds even though they're no longer earning interest. And in 1995, the rules changed again. The government will no longer guarantee a minimum interest rate, so the rates on savings bond will be completely linked to fluctuations in the Treasury's other rates.

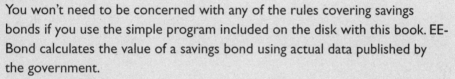
EEBond on the Disk

You won't need to be concerned with any of the rules covering savings bonds if you use the simple program included on the disk with this book. EE-Bond calculates the value of a savings bond using actual data published by the government.

To run this program, you need to be running DOS, not Windows. A file in the root directory of the disk, called "readme.txt," will guide you through the process of installing EEBond and getting started with the program.

To find the value of a savings bond in EEBond, you first need to create a new file. Type Alt-F to open the file menu and give your new file a name. Then, enter details on each of the bonds you own. To see a snapshot of the value of the bond, press Alt-F5, or select Cumulative Reports from the Report menu. You'll see the current value of the bond, the face value of the bonds and the total interest earned. Any bonds that no longer earn interest are marked with an asterisk. As you enter bonds, this report will show the total for all of your holdings. If you want to see the status of a single bond, you need to create a new file, enter just the details for that bond and then open the cumulative report. If you want to add bonds to an existing file, press F8 or select Edit from the Data menu.

The Treasury Department publishes a new table of interest rates twice a year, in May and October. The version EEBond on this book's disk is accurate through May 1995. For an update with newer data, follow the instructions in the disk file README.TXT. You'll receive a free update by return mail. EEBond is shareware; if you use the program, you should register with the author and pay for it. You'll also receive additional updates if you register.

Whether you already own savings bonds or are considering purchasing them, you'll want to give this program a try. Look for it in the directory \CHAPTER.6 under Shareware and More.

Calculating the value of savings bonds

Dollar amount on the bond

Date bond purchased

Indicat[e] bond is no long[er] earning interes[t]

How muc[h] bond will cashed in

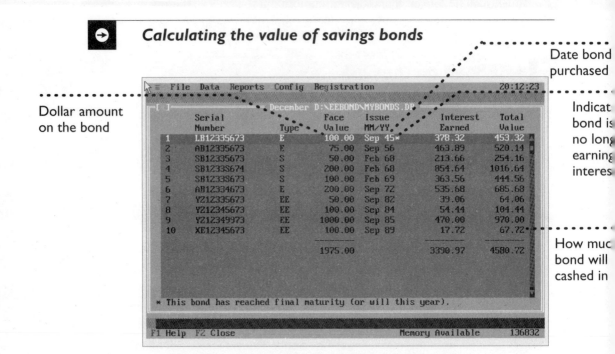

	Serial Number	Type	Face Value	Issue MM/YY	Interest Earned	Total Value
1	LB12335673	E	100.00	Sep 45*	378.32	453.32
2	AB12335673	E	75.00	Sep 56	463.89	520.14
3	SB12335673	S	50.00	Feb 68	213.66	254.16
4	SB1233S674	S	200.00	Feb 68	854.64	1016.64
5	SB1233S673	S	100.00	Feb 69	363.56	444.56
6	AB12334673	E	200.00	Sep 72	535.68	685.68
7	Y21Z335673	EE	50.00	Sep 82	39.06	64.06
8	Y212345673	EE	100.00	Sep 84	54.44	104.44
9	Y212349973	EE	1000.00	Sep 85	470.00	970.00
10	XE12345673	EE	100.00	Sep 89	17.72	67.72
			1975.00		3390.97	4580.72

File Data Reports Config Registration   20:12:23

December D:\EEBOND\MYBONDS.DP

* This bond has reached final maturity (or will this year).

F1 Help   F2 Close   Memory Available   136832

7 | Protecting Your Kingdom

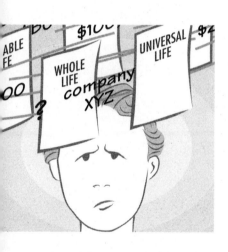

106 Assessing Your Life Insurance Needs

110 Shopping for a Life Insurance Policy

116 Creating a Home Inventory

Your home computer may not provide the same sense of security that you'll get from keeping strong locks on your doors, living a healthy lifestyle, and wearing seat belts. But there are a few tools on your computer that you can use to help safeguard your home and family.

You want to be sure you have enough insurance to reimburse you for any losses, but you don't want to waste money by buying protection that you don't need. And you want to make every effort to be able to collect on insurance that you already own. This chapter will show you how to used computer-based tools to do the following:

- ✔ Assess your life insurance needs
- ✔ Shop for a life insurance policy
- ✔ Create a home inventory
- ✔ Build a home inventory spreadsheet

It will also show you how to make sure you'll be able to collect when you do incur losses.

In 1995, insurance companies will be experimenting with online sales for insurance policies. If these early trials are successful, you'll eventually be able to buy all types of insurance with your computer. For the next few years, however, plan on buying insurance only after visiting with an agent. But before you sit down, you'll be better prepared to buy the right amount of insurance if you've tried out the following techniques for assessing your need for life insurance, and homeowner's insurance.

Assessing Your Life Insurance Needs

Before you buy life insurance, it's important to remember the reason for having it. Life insurance must provide protection for your survivors so they can carry on in the event you die. If you have no dependents, you don't need life insurance. If your spouse could very easily earn enough to support the family, your needs for life insurance are minimal, although your planning must explore contingencies, such as the need for childcare after one parent dies. When buying life insurance, you should not try to provide an income for your survivors for the rest of their lives (unless they're incapable of supporting themselves), but you should provide enough so that children can complete college, your spouse won't need to sell the house, and everyone in the family will have enough money for a transition that will last several years. Only after you've taken all of that into account are you ready to decide on the amount of coverage you need.

Assessing life insurance needs with a spreadsheet

Sit down at your computer before you see an agent.

The formulas entered to achieve the results in the spreadsheet at left

A spreadsheet can help. The spreadsheet on this page shows one way. In essence, it lists expenses your survivors will be likely to face, totals them all up, and then compares the totals to your savings and Social Security benefits. Among the expenses you'll want to include is paying off all loans and mortgages, so the family can keep living in the same house. Then, annual expenses must be estimated. In this spreadsheet, whenever there are single sums—such as the size of the current mortgage—they're entered as a lump sum. But for calculating expenses like medical insurance, it's easier to take whichever figures are certain and then multiply them by a time period. In the example here, needs were calculated for 10 years. (Since financial needs vary from one family to another, there's no way of creating a universal version of this spreadsheet, so you will not find one on the accompanying CD-ROM.)

Don't forget to include Social Security survivor's benefits. While the amount varies based on a wage-earner's contributions, most families can count on some monthly benefit. You'll find a chart on this page with a range of values for various situations. The amount of benefit that the Social Security Administration pays is based on the amount of tax paid into your account. Workers with high earnings who've paid into the system for years are entitled to greater benefits than workers with fewer years and lower levels of contributions. The maximum death benefit payment to a family is $2,162 monthly.

What Social Security Pays to Survivors

This table shows sample death benefits for someone who regularly contributed to the Social Security system (based on 1993 SSA figures).

Worker	Salary at Death	Monthly Social Security Payment
35-year-old with spouse and one child	$30,000	$1,506
35-year-old with spouse and two children	$50,000	$2,182
45-year-old with spouse and one child	$30,000	$1,504
45-year-old with spouse and two children	$30,000	$2,112
55-year-old with spouse and one child	$30,000	$1,490
55-year-old with spouse and two children	$30,000	$1,986

If creating a spreadsheet is too much work, you may want to take advantage of a wonderful tool in Managing Your Money, a software program from Meca. It helps you calculate the amount of insurance you'll need. Managing Your Money can perform many of the chores that Quicken does. I haven't discussed it much because it's not nearly as good as Quicken at paying bills and tracking your spending. But among the several valuable tools in Managing Your Money are calculators that ask you to provide personal details and then help you make decisions about life insurance purchases.

You'll find the life insurance calculators on Managing Your Money's Plan menu. Here you'll also find a Life Expectancy tool, an amusing bit of software that will ask you personal questions, including whether you smoke, how often you exercise and whether you wear a seat belt. After you've provided personal information, it calculates your life expectancy based on published actuarial tables. The program concludes with the wise advice that no matter how long you're expected to live, you should still buy life insurance, just in case.

Estimating life insurance needs with Managing Your Money

The software can calculate the amount for different scenarios.

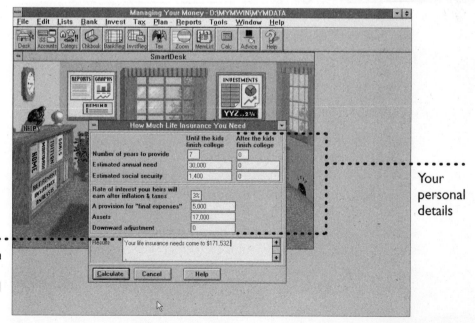

Your personal details

How much coverage you should have

Managing Your Money's next tool for life insurance helps you estimate the amount you need. It assumes you have children and asks you to estimate the number of years before your children complete college and the number of years thereafter that you want to continue to provide. Feel free to change numbers over and over so the software can calculate the amount for different scenarios. One benefit of using the calculator is that it shows your estimated Social Security benefit (you will only be eligible for these benefits if the government has collected its tax from your earnings over the years). One area where the program is of no help is in projecting the needs of your survivors. If you've created your own spreadsheet, you'll be in better shape to answer the question here.

Whether you use a spreadsheet or not, you can benefit from another Managing Your Money calculator, which estimates how much insurance should cost. The software asks for your age, sex, and whether you're a smoker. Then it displays an estimate of term life insurance premiums. I've found the program's estimates to be on the high side, but shopping for life insurance prices is hard work, so you'll probably find it valuable to have this estimate before you talk to agents.

Shopping for a Life Insurance Policy

Shopping for a life insurance policy can be confusing. Agents will try to convince you of the merits of whole life, variable life and universal life insurance policies. The policy they're least likely to advocate is term life insurance. A term policy is the only type of insurance that is strictly a life insurance policy. All other policies combine life insurance with a form of investments and are usually classified as permanent life insurance.

Insurance companies have created many variations, but the basic concept is that permanent insurance policies guarantee you'll pay a fixed premium every year, while term policy premiums increase every year. For example, a 35-year-old male may be able to buy $100,000 of whole life and pay $1,100 a year for as long as he lives. The same 35-year-old male could buy $100,000 of term insurance for about $150, but he'll be faced with higher premiums every year. When he's in his sixties, he'll be paying about $1,500 to maintain the same $100,000 policy.

How much should life insurance cost?

Let your computer do some of the work before you talk to an agent.

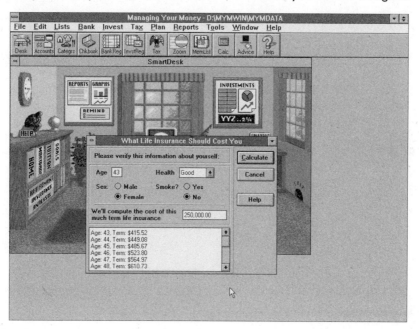

Term policies provide only a death benefit to the survivors named in the policy. Permanent policies pay a death benefit, too, but they also pay dividends to the policyholder and have a cash value (if you terminate the policy before you die, you receive a percentage of the amount you've paid in). Choosing a policy can be very difficult because insurance companies have different approaches to the dividends and cash values they pay; you're not just shopping for the best price among insurance companies, you're also comparing products that have different provisions. Universal and variable life insurance are permanent policies that have flexible premiums and benefits, based on changes in market conditions.

→ *It's all so confusing.*

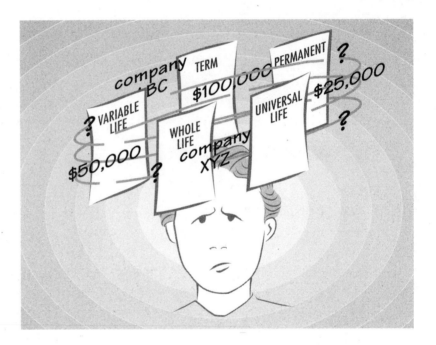

Basic Types of Life Insurance

Type	Description
Term	Pays a specified amount in the event the policyholder dies during the term of the policy. Must be renewed at fixed intervals. Premiums will steadily increase with age.
Permanent	An umbrella term for several types of insurance that combine term life insurance with investments. Specific types include whole life, universal life, and variable life.
Universal life	Premiums will vary based on changes in interest rates. The policyholder can decide to pay more or less than the initial premium, changing the amount of coverage. Cash value will change based on changes in interest rates.

Basic Types of Life Insurance (Continued)

Type	Description
Variable life	Premiums can be fixed or flexible. Cash value and death benefit vary according to the performance of investments. Policyholders have some control over where the premiums are invested.
Whole life	Premiums are set at the beginning of the policy and never change. The policy pays a specified amount in the event the policyholder dies during the term of the policy. Can be cashed in at any time for a percentage of the total value, which increases each year. Dividends are usually paid every year.

Analyzing insurance choices

Your computer can help you start thinking straight.

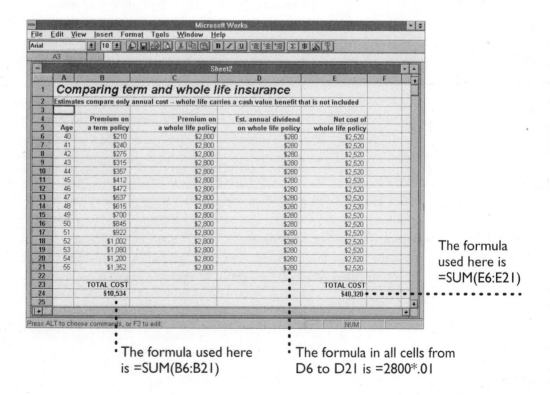

The formula used here is =SUM(E6:E21)

The formula used here is =SUM(B6:B21)

The formula in all cells from D6 to D21 is =2800*.01

After a visit with a life insurance agent, your head will probably be spinning with questions. One way to help you start thinking straight is to put the numbers into a spreadsheet. The example on this page shows how you can use a spreadsheet to compare the cost of a term and a whole life policy. (You'll find a copy of this spreadsheet on the CD-ROM that comes with this book. Look for the file TERM_WHO.WK1 in the directory \CHAPTER.7 under Worksheets.) Premiums on the term policy change each year; an insurance agent will provide you with the premiums charged by his or her company, or you can use the estimates that Managing Your Money's insurance costs calculator displays.

➔ Comparing Costs with a Spreadsheet

To build the spreadsheet, the amount for each premium on the term policy had to be entered by hand (using figures supplied by an insurance agent). The premium for the whole life policy was entered just once. It doesn't vary, so I copied the number and pasted it into all of the other cells. The dividend is an estimate based on an insurance agent's assertion that the whole life policy will pay at least a 10 percent premium. Calculating this is easy: I used a formula that multiplies the value in the whole life premium cell by .1 (for 10 percent). Since a dividend can be used to reduce the cost of a premium, column E calculates the net cost, which is the premium minus the dividend.

In this example, I've totaled up the cost for all term policy and whole life premiums based on holding the policy from the age of 40 to age 55. Other factors will need to be assessed as well. The whole life policy has a cash value starting in the third year. The cash value in the first year is about $3,300; in the second year, it's about $5,800 and goes up each year.

➔ Comparing Costs with a Spreadsheet

To fairly compare the two types of insurance, you will want to include the whole life policy's cash value in your projections, but since it changes every year, you can only perform the calculation at the point you want to cash in the policy. For example, if you cashed it in during the fifth year, your comparison would look like the spreadsheet on the following page. (You'll find a copy of this spreadsheet on the companion CD-ROM. Look for the file T_W_CASH.WK1 in the directory \CHAPTER.7 under Worksheets.) You can easily create this spreadsheet if you start with the original spreadsheet that compares the two policies. First, delete rows after the period you're examining. Then, add a SUM formula to total all of the premiums for both the term and whole life policies. Now, subtract the cash value payment from the whole life policies to see how much it really cost you to have protection for four years. Be sure to save this spreadsheet with a different name so you don't overwrite the original spreadsheet.

Checklist for Life Insurance Shopping

✔ Determine the amount of coverage you need
✔ Decide whether you want a term policy or a permanent policy
✔ Shop by talking to agents
✔ Check the financial stability of the company before you buy

Before buying insurance, check the financial stability of the company. Insurance companies are rated by Standard & Poors. You can call them and ask for a company's rating (the service is free, though you must call their New York office at 212-208-1527 during business hours). The highest rating is AAA and steps down to AA until it reaches CCC. Avoid companies lower than AA.

What if you cash in the policy?

Comparing the returns from term and whole life

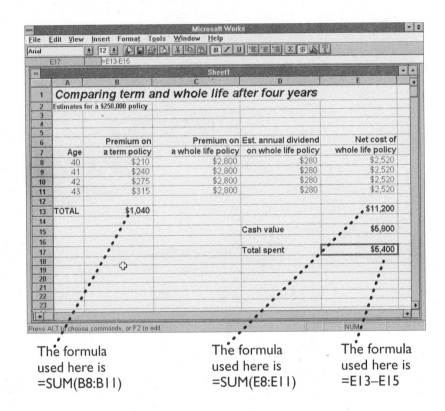

	The formula used here is =SUM(B8:B11)		The formula used here is =SUM(E8:E11)	The formula used here is =E13–E15

Creating a Home Inventory

The best way to cope with disaster is to know what you have. Creating a home inventory isn't the most fun you'll ever have with your computer, but it could turn out to be the most important thing you do with it. After a fire, flood, or theft, few people are thinking clearly enough to deal with the insurance paperwork properly. The main purpose of creating a home inventory now should be obvious: to have a written record of what you owned to help you file an insurance claim or police report.

But an inventory will also help you get an accurate picture of what your home is really worth. You probably bought your homeowner's policy when the house was empty and you were thinking only of the resale value of the building and land. After you've spent a few years carting things home from the mall one trip at a time, the only way you can be sure of knowing what you really have is to follow the same accepted accounting procedure practiced by businesses everywhere: You've got to take an inventory, item by item.

Aside from putting yourself in a good position to file a claim on your homeowner's policy if it ever becomes necessary, you'll also learn how much your possessions are worth. Many people will find after tallying up the value of their possessions that they're not carrying enough homeowner's insurance. And, insurance agents will tell you that when it comes time to file a claim, most people underestimate the value of their personal belongings. As a result, they cheat themselves because they don't remember what was lost. If you've never taken an inventory, you'll be amazed at how much all of that stuff in your house is really worth.

An inventory will help you get an accurate picture of what your home is really worth.

The deluxe version of Quicken includes a home inventory tool that will help you create a record of everything in your home. But I've found that it's faster to create your own spreadsheet. Quicken can slow you down by presenting you with so many options. If you're prepared to devote several hours to the task of recording a home inventory and have neatly organized files with many receipts, and all of your insurance policies, Quicken's Home Inventory will be a good guide through the process. But in my view, you'll record far more information and put in more work than necessary using Quicken. For example, Quicken asks you to supply a replacement cost and a resale value; both of these items will change over time, and you'll need to update them periodically. Simply recording the amount you paid for merchandise is sufficient for a home inventory. If you have the time and energy to supply these values for all of your home possessions, it's worth doing. Most of us, however, are lucky to find the time to create any records at all.

It's easy to forget how much you have invested in your home.

Using your computer for an inventory will help you remember.

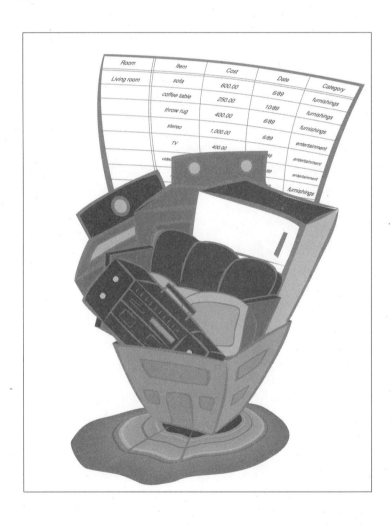

Quicken Home Inventory does provide other benefits. It will summarize all of the items you've entered, assign them to insurance policies, and then compare the total of your possessions against the value of your policy. You can also have Quicken generate a claim report if you incur a loss, a dubious benefit since your insurance company will require that you complete their forms as well. People who will benefit from using Quicken are homeowners with many assets and plenty of time.

I also don't like the fact that Quicken's inventory is locked into a computer file format that only Quicken can open. Disaster recovery plans must be flexible—you can't assume that you'll be using your computer when you most need the information in your inventory. While you should keep a printed version of your inventory, you also will want to keep a backup of the file, and the file should be usable on many computers. A spreadsheet file, whether generated in Microsoft Works, Lotus 1-2-3, or Microsoft Excel, can be saved in a text format that can be read on any computer.

> *Disaster recovery plans must be flexible—you can't assume that you'll be using your computer when you most need the information in your inventory.*

If you're like most people, creating a home inventory is not high on your list of ways to spend the weekend. So you'll want to complete the task as quickly as possible. The best way to get the job done fast is to use either a spreadsheet or a word processor. A spreadsheet is the better tool if you're comfortable using one. But completing a home inventory is an important enough job that if you don't own Quicken Deluxe and you're not comfortable using a spreadsheet, you should use a word processor to make a simple list of everything in the house, with your best recollection of what you paid for it. Make a backup copy of this list on a floppy disk, and make at least two copies of a printed version of the list.

If you are comfortable using a spreadsheet, the following steps will help you finish the job quickly and provide you with records that should prove extremely valuable if you need to file a claim. You can use the spreadsheet on this book's

CD-ROM to get a head start. (The spreadsheet is called HOME_CAT.WK1 and it's in the directory \CHAPTER.7 under Worksheets).

Any spreadsheet program can be used to build a home inventory. In its most basic form, all you need to do is create a list of items in your home, assign a dollar value to each, and then add other information that may be useful in organizing the information and in helping you remember details about items that could be controversial in a claim. After you've tallied up everything, a simple SUM formula will add up all of the individual dollar values and show you the total value of your possessions. If you want to divide your possessions into categories, you can put in a little more effort. The most important task to accomplish is getting a complete list in writing. Once you've done that, you can embellish the inventory if you wish.

→ Building a Home Inventory Spreadsheet

The following explanation will help you accomplish the basics first. If you run out of time, you don't need to finish the later steps.

Start by opening a new spreadsheet. In the first cell, type "room." In the cell to its right, type "item." Now you're ready to start entering everything in the house (if you use the spreadsheet on the disk you can skip this step, since the work was already done for you). You want to be systematic, so select a room near the front entrance and enter the name under "room." Select Copy from the Edit menu, move your cursor to the cell directly below and select Paste from the edit menu. Do this until you have at least 10 copies of the room name. Record everything in the room according to where it's sitting. Now, take a walk through that room and look around; you'll find many more items that you forgot to enter. Return to the computer and fill in what's missing.

Next, repeat the procedure for a room that's adjacent to the first room and continue room by room, until you've included the entire house. Don't forget the garage, attic, laundry rooms—every place that contains something of value. When you add a room, enter each closet as a separate room; it will help you be more specific.

➔ *Building a Home Inventory Spreadsheet*

After you've recorded all of your possessions—or at least made a healthy start—create at least three more columns. Next to items, create a column where you'll record the cost. If you have records, you can use them, but it's better to record a rough estimate than nothing. To help give the list more credibility—and to help you recall details later—create a column that shows where you bought the item or the source if it was a gift. Next, create a column for the date when you obtained it; that will help if the insurance company wants to depreciate the item. The basic rule is the more information you have, the better. But you don't need to make yourself crazy by puzzling over exact dates.

Finally, you may want to add a column that identifies each item by category. This isn't needed for filing insurance claims, but can help you plan a budget or settle an argument with your spouse. Do this only if you're the type who likes to analyze. How much do you really have tied up in electronics? Sorting by categories will allow you to classify each item as clothing, furniture, and so on. After you've successfully entered everything by room, you can then sort all of the items by category. The easiest way to do this is to create categories that interest you and then assign a letter to each. Make the category identifiers easy to remember. To see your inventory sorted by category, select the Sort command (in Microsoft Works you find it on the Tools menu). Be sure you sort only the cells that list items—don't sort the total!

After you've got a fair number of items, reward yourself by having the spreadsheet create a total for the value of everything. Enter the total far down the sheet. If you enter the formula in row 60 and you're using Microsoft Works, the formula you'll use is =SUM(C1:C59).

To see the total, you'll need to split the sheet. Make sure your cursor is sitting on the fourth row from the bottom before you choose the split screen command. You don't want to split the screen in half; you just want to devote about three rows of the screen to the total so you have plenty of room to continue entering data in the top half. In Microsoft Works, the Split command is on the Window menu. When you feel you've recorded the majority of your possessions, compare the total value with the amount covered by your homeowner's or apartment renter's policy.

After you've accomplished the basic job of recording an inventory of all your possessions, you can use the spreadsheet to keep track of warranties. Simply create additional columns. Enter details about warranties for any item where it applies. Serial numbers should be recorded on items like bicycles and electronics equipment.

The spreadsheet list will be helpful if you ever need to file a loss claim, but you should also create a video tape showing your possessions, room by room. Walk through the house and explain what you're seeing, then store the tape in a safe deposit box. The videotape isn't going to have values entered, and it won't show what's tucked into the closets so the spreadsheet is a good complement. And an advantage to the spreadsheet is that it's easy to create multiple copies.

It should take less than an hour to build the sheet. Then, print several copies and copy it to at least one floppy disk—in both the native spreadsheet format and in a text format—and keep copies of it in several places: a safe deposit box, a metal box in the attic, and your office.

The most important thing to remember about a home inventory is that any inventory is better than none. Don't make your plan so elaborate that you spend all your time designing it—with no time left to carry it out.

8

Shopping for Loans and Mortgages

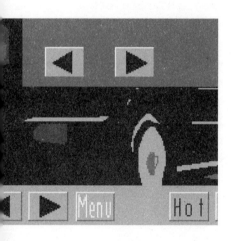

127 The New Car Decision: A
Spreadsheet Can Help

135 Buying a House: Figuring
What You Can Afford

138 Shopping for Mortgages

We all need to be prepared to take on debt at some time. Taking on a larger debt than you can manage is a sure way to financial ruin, but if you're careful and make certain your monthly payments fit within your budget, a loan is a smart way to pay for a car, an apartment, or a house. A loan can be more than a fast way to get the things you want, it can help you increase your net worth if you take on debt carefully. A home mortgage is considered the best investment the average family can make: The interest on a home mortgage is tax deductible, and the value of the home will appreciate if it's held long enough. Since you need to spend money on housing one way or the other, you're better off investing in your home instead of renting.

Large loans, especially car loans and mortgages, will have a dramatic affect on your personal finances, so you'll want to be prepared before you sign a loan agreement. Shopping carefully for car financing can save you thousands of dollars; shopping carefully for an apartment or home mortgage can save you tens of thousands of dollars.

A credit card is the first experience many of us have with the discipline of borrowing money and paying it back on time (or as close to it as we can manage). In Chapter 3 ("Making Credit Cards Work for You"), we discussed credit cards and how to keep them under control. Credit cards have a significant benefit beyond instant gratification. Regular use of a credit card builds a credit history that lenders will evaluate when you apply for any type of loan. So if you're not yet ready to apply for a car or home mortgage, you can put yourself in a better position to apply for one in the future by using credit cards regularly—and paying off the balance on time (some mortgage lenders will ask that you explain any late payments—even years later).

This chapter will help you navigate the bracing waters of lending. We'll focus on buying a car and a house, but the techniques apply to any type of loan. In this chapter we'll show you how to use spreadsheets and other tools to do the following:

- ✔ Figure the true costs of a loan
- ✔ Evaluate whether buying or leasing a car is better for you
- ✔ Determine what a car should cost
- ✔ Figure what size mortgage you can afford
- ✔ Shop for a mortgage

One of the most valuable skills you can have as you decide on whether you should accept the terms of a loan is the ability to create a spreadsheet that accurately reveals the cost to you. As we look at the decision to buy a car and a house, you'll see how to build spreadsheets that you can customize to reflect your own special needs.

The New Car Decision: A Spreadsheet Can Help

Financing your new car isn't a simple process. First you have to haggle on a price with the dealer, and then you've got to decide how you'll pay for the car. Whatever you do, don't buy a car without crunching the numbers through your own spreadsheet. The dealer will try to present the numbers in a way that's dealer-approved. With a spreadsheet, you'll be able to understand your options better. The same spreadsheet can help you choose the car and options you want to buy and also how to pay for it.

For too many people, all that matters in a car deal is the number they'll be writing on a check now and each month: If they can afford the amount and want the car, they go ahead. Instead, you should consider whether you're getting the best deal you can. A properly crafted spreadsheet can take the facts and figures in the car deal and help you evaluate whether you're making the right move.

The first goal of your spreadsheet is to help you get a handle on the "options" that can add thousands to the purchase price of a car. Option packages are deceptive. For example, you think of it as just buying a radio, but if it's part of a package, you may not realize that it's costing you over $1,000 because the dealer includes other options, which you may not even want. When you itemize on your spreadsheet, the cost is obvious. Your spreadsheet will also help you consider the cost of items like taxes and destination charges.

The most important choice to evaluate is whether to buy the car with a loan or to lease it. A loan is actually a purchase of the car, with a little help from your bank. In a lease, you never take legal possession of the car; it is owned by the

➡ Are you getting a good deal?

No matter what the dealer says, don't buy a car before crunching the numbers through your own spreadsheet.

➡ Quicken's Loan Calculator: A Shortcut

If you already own Quicken, you might be tempted to rely on the loan calculator you'll find on the program's Plan menu. It's easy to use and seems to give you all the help you need in planning for a loan.

While Quicken's calculator does report the amount of a loan payment, based on the amount borrowed, interest rate, and term, you can do this very easily yourself in a spreadsheet. The examples in this chapter show you how, using a PMT (payment) function in a spreadsheet. The advantage of a spreadsheet is that it can include all of the factors in the amount you're going to borrow. For example, in a car purchase, you may not be sure of the amount you need to borrow; a spreadsheet can help you decide how much you can afford by looking at all of the factors in a car purchase. When you add and subtract options from the car's total price, you see how much that will affect your monthly payment.

lease company, and you must return it at the end of the term. You may have a preference for either buying or leasing based on whether you like holding on to a car or not, but if you're interested in the financial aspect of this decision, you'll probably find a spreadsheet to be an invaluable help.

The same spreadsheet that helped you decide on the options you wanted can now help you choose the financing option. In the spreadsheet you see on this page, the top rows list the price of the car and options. The spreadsheet is designed to calculate the sales tax on the total amount and then to calculate costs for both leasing and buying the car with a loan.

CARBUY.WK1 is a spreadsheet on this book's companion CD-ROM that you can use to evaluate a car purchase. (It's located in the \CHAPTER.8 directory under Worksheets.) By replacing the prices in this example with your own figures, you'll be in a better position to know exactly what a car will cost you and it will help you decide between buying and leasing a car. All of the figures you should replace are indicated by an arrow; the other figures are calculated by formulas.

The spreadsheet is designed to be used after doing a little shopping, either by browsing online or by visiting car showrooms. The first figure entered is the base price of the car without any options. Next, each option and the destination charges are listed. With all of the separate charges listed, we can perform a total (in row 6) and on that total, we can calculate the sales tax. Sales tax is identified separately from the total because it's treated differently depending on whether it's by a lease or a loan. In a lease, the sales tax is not paid at the time of purchase; you pay tax each month on the lease payment. When you buy a car with a loan, sales tax is paid at the time of the sale. The amount you borrow includes sales tax.

The spreadsheet now splits into two separate columns because once the price of the car is set, you calculate a loan and a lease differently. Before you can calculate the monthly payments, you need to take into account what you pay up front. In a lease, it's usually called the capital cost reduction, but other names are also used. In a loan, it's called the down payment. The total amount leased or borrowed is reduced by this amount.

Lease or buy?

Help in deciding between buying or leasing a car

.All figures next to an arrow
are figures you must enter.
All other figures are calculated
in the spreadsheet.

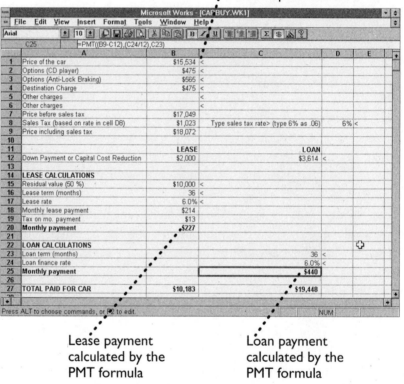

Lease payment
calculated by the
PMT formula

Loan payment
calculated by the
PMT formula

A lease calculation starts with the price of the car, minus the capital reduction cost and minus the residual value of the car. The residual value is the price the lease company expects the car will be worth after the lease ends. If the lease company places a fair residual value on the car, the lease is likely to be a good deal; but the lease company may expect the car to drop in value drastically, which means you'll be expected to pay most of the sticker price during the lease term.

➜ How Much Should That Car Really Cost?

Buying a car can be a stressful chore. You feel compelled to negotiate with a dealer, and you're on unfamiliar ground. You're sitting at his desk and he's got stacks of intimidating papers, but all you know is what he's told you. You're sure other people know how to get a better price, but how?

You'll be better equipped to negotiate for a car if you know one of the numbers the dealer knows: the price the dealer must pay to the car manufacturer. This figure, called the "dealer invoice cost," is published by a service called AutoNet—and you can find it with either CompuServe or Prodigy.

➜ What does a new car cost your dealer?

Use AutoNet to find out.

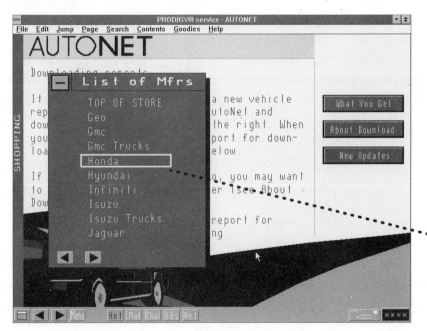

AutoNet's database includes most popular models currently on sale.

→ How Much Should That Car Really Cost?

AutoNet also lists the details on 44 specs (such as the amount of head-room, engine displacement, and steering diameter) and the availability of 31 different options (ranging from power windows to leather seats). You will find both the suggested list price of options and the dealer's cost.

Advertising slogans notwithstanding, no car dealer is willing to give away a car, so you won't be able to buy a car for less than the dealer invoice cost (unless you're shopping after the model year is over and the manufacturer is offering discounts to dealers). You can assume the dealer is willing to sell the car for a price somewhere between the car's sticker price and the dealer invoice cost.

To find AutoNet on CompuServe, type GO NEWCAR from any Compu-Serve prompt; each report costs about 90 cents. Before you view the re-port, be prepared to either print it or save it to a disk file, since you'll want to refer to it later. To find AutoNet on Prodigy, use the Jumpword AUTONET. Prodigy does not let you view the report while you're con-nected but it makes the process of downloading the report to your com-puter very easy. Prodigy's reports cost about $4 but they usually include all of the variations in a model (4-door, 2-door, hatchback, and so on); CompuServe's reports cost less but you may need to download several with separate charges for each in order to do a complete evaluation of your choices.

A loan is often the better deal because lease residual values are too low for a basic reason: A residual value represents what a used car dealer will pay for the car in the expectation of making a profit. So the residual value is usually about 5 to 15 percent below a car's true market value, which is what a consumer is will-ing to pay.

These factors are typical, but lease companies have many variations. Some require security deposits. Others ask for the last month's payment up front. You'll have to change the spreadsheet to reflect the terms that have been offered to you. Because deals like lease and loan arrangements can vary so much, it's worth learning how to build a spreadsheet like this so you'll be able to break down the sales talk into hard numbers—if you don't understand a figure in the lease agreement, ask for an explanation. The process of making your spreadsheet work will guarantee that you understand the obligation you're taking on. It will also help to slow you down: Rushing into a major purchase is never a good idea.

The interest rate and the term of the agreement are similar in a lease or a loan, so you'll find the next few lines of the spreadsheet similar for the loan and lease.

While it's quite common for leases to be offered on specific models, this is a sales tactic. Dealers have fully equipped models they're trying to move, and they claim it's at a special price. The only way you can be sure if the price is really a discount is to compare the dealer's price with the published option prices (which you can download from AutoNet or find in new car price books sold at newsstands).

➜ *A Quick Lesson in Spreadsheet Formulas*

If you've never entered a spreadsheet formula, the need to evaluate a large loan is an excellent reason to learn. Your spreadsheet's help system or manual will have details, but here's a quick summary of how it works.

Most spreadsheet cells contain text or numbers, but cells that contain formulas perform operations on other cells. The first character in the formula is a symbol identifying this cell's contents as a formula. In Microsoft Works and Microsoft Excel, an equal sign (=) begins every formula. In Lotus 1-2-3, a "care-of" or at sign (@) begins every formula. The next words represent the operation to be performed. PMT is the beginning of a "payment" formula for calculating the amount to be paid on a loan agreement.

➜ A Quick Lesson in Spreadsheet Formulas

After the formula is identified, a string of entries, bracketed by parentheses, must appear next. The entries and their exact order are specified in the spreadsheet's help system. In a payment formula, the structure of the formula is to list the amount of the loan, the interest rate, and the number of payments. An entry can be either a specific value (the price of the car) or other cells in the spreadsheet (where the price is stored); each entry is separated by a comma. The PMT formula requires that interest rates be correct for each period, so in a typical loan arrangement where the interest rate is based on an annual term, the interest rate must be divided by 12.

Entries can be a combination of more than one value or cell; for example, the car price minus the amount of the down payment. Such flexibility allows you to construct a single formula to handle countless changes, for example, purchase price, interest rate, and loan term. The formula takes it all in stride, showing new results every time you change a variable.

The spreadsheet on the disk will let you change any of the values, such as prices, interest rates, and loan terms. But it will stop you from changing entries where formulas make the calculation, such as totals of prices and calculation of the payments (PMT). Most people won't need to change these formulas, although you may need to add rows to include more options or other lease charges. You can do that by inserting rows. If you need to change the formulas, you'll need to open the spreadsheet's protect command and change the status of the cells from protected to unprotected. In Microsoft Works, the protect command is on the Format menu.

In using the spreadsheet, be sure to enter interest rates as a percentage. For example, an 8 percent interest rate is entered as .08. And loan terms should be entered as months; a three-year term is 36 months.

What the payment formula means

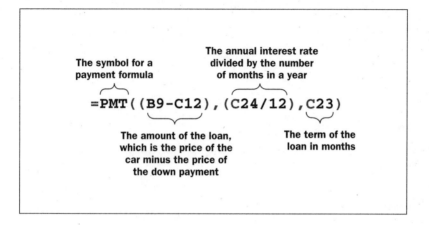

There isn't a simple answer to the question of whether a loan or lease makes better sense for you. In the final analysis, the value of the car at the end of the term is central to determining which is a better deal. If you feel the car will hold its value well after the lease term ends, you're better off taking out a loan and buying the car. For most people, a lease costs significantly more. Remember that after you return the car to the lease company, you'll need another car. Payments on a loan may be higher, but in time, you'll pay off the loan and still have the car.

Buying a House: Figuring What You Can Afford

Buying a home is a learning process, but unfortunately, many people learn how much they can afford—and how much they'll have to pay—after they've fallen in love with a house. Traditionally, home buyers have relied on a bank loan officer to learn how much of a mortgage they could afford. You'll be much better off if you do the calculations yourself, before you invest too much energy in house hunting.

Calculate before you look

Calculate what you can afford *before* you start looking for a house.

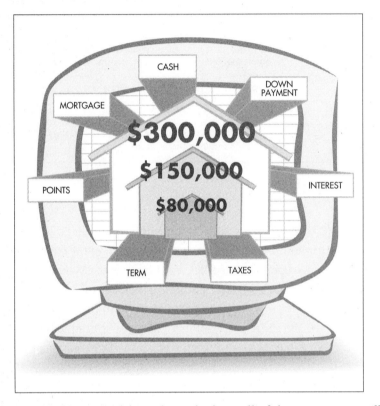

 It's fairly easy to build a spreadsheet that calculates all of the expenses you'll incur in buying a home. The companion CD-ROM to this book includes MORTGAGE.WK1 (in the directory \CHAPTER.8 under Worksheets), a spreadsheet you can use immediately to estimate the cost of buying a home.

The spreadsheet is designed to help with two key factors: the cash you'll need to close the deal and the monthly payment you'll be committed to make for the life of your mortgage. Many first-time buyers are unprepared for the size of the closing costs and often get far into the deal before they realize how much more they need. While exact amounts vary because of local and state regulations, closing costs range from $3,000 to $10,000 for the average home.

The spreadsheet on disk can give you a realistic estimate of these costs. Many are difficult to predict, so our spreadsheet is based on the higher range. A real estate broker may be of some help, but because a broker has a vested interest in making you feel good about buying the home, it's best to find someone with less of a conflict, such as an attorney with experience in closing home purchases in your area. A good attorney will do his or her best to make certain the closing goes smoothly, and helping you prepare for the closing costs is one part of the job. For example, the attorney can recommend ways to avoid paying some of the costs. A survey may not be needed if the seller can supply a recent survey and no major changes have been made to the property.

The spreadsheet is designed to show you the full cost of a home purchase, based on all of the variables: the price of the house, the size of the mortgage, the mortgage interest rate, points on the loan, the length of the mortgage, the size of the down payment, and the property taxes. To help you use this spreadsheet, right arrows appear to the right of all of the cells where you should enter your own figures. Other cells are formulas and while you can change them if you want to use different assumptions (such as a higher down payment percentage), you will first need to unprotect the cells from the spreadsheet's menus.

The spreadsheet is designed to simplify the calculation by placing the most important information at the top. After you enter the price and mortgage information, the spreadsheet will make the calculations and report the figures that matter most: the cash you'll need and the monthly payment after you move in.

Learning how to customize the spreadsheet can help you in many related situations. A second mortgage (or home equity loan), for instance, is similar to a first mortgage except the closing costs are dramatically different. A look at the formulas behind the home-buyer's worksheet shows that the structure of the spreadsheet is very simple to understand. You'll find all of the entries to the left of arrows are numbers you can change. The other cells are formulas you should be able to understand by referring to the quick lesson in spreadsheet formulas earlier in this chapter.

Adding up closing costs

Many first-time buyers are unprepared for this aspect of the purchase.

```
┌──────────────────────────────────────────────────────────────────────────┐
│           Microsoft Works - [MORTGAGE.WK1]                         ▼ ▲    │
│  File  Edit  View  Insert  Format  Tools  Window  Help                    ▲│
│ Arial          ± 10 ±                                              Σ $    ▲│
│       E3           =PMT(B5,(B6/12),(B8*12))+E2                              │
```

	A	B	C	D	E	F	G
1	Cash needed to buy a house	$44,850		Monthly loan payment	$1,076		
2				Monthly escrow (taxes)	$333		
3	COST OF HOME & MORTGAGE			Total monthly payment	$1,410		
4	Price of the house	$175,000	<				
5	Mortgage Amount	$140,000	<				
6	Mortgage Interest Rate	8.50%	<				
7	Points Charged by Lender	2	<				
8	Loan Term	30	<				
9	Annual Real Estate Taxes	$4,000	<				
10	Contract Deposit	$17,500					
11							
12	CLOSING COSTS						
13	Down payment at closing	$17,500					
14	Inspection of house	$350	<				
15	Mortgage Insurance	$650	<				
16	Attorney's fee	$4,000	<				
17	Loan origination fee	$750	<				
18	Recording fee	$100	<				
19	Appraisal	$300	<			⊕	
20	Loan application fee	$300	<				
21	Survey	$300	<				
22	Title search and insurance	$600	<				
23	Homeowner's insurance	$1,000	<				
24	State and local transfer tax	$1,500	<				
25	Other costs		<				
26							
27	TOTAL CLOSING COSTS	$27,350					

```
│ Press ALT to choose commands, or F2 to edit.                      NUM      │
└──────────────────────────────────────────────────────────────────────────┘
```

The cash needed includes a down payment and closing costs.

All figures next to an arrow are costs you must enter. The other figures are calculated by the spreadsheet.

Shopping for Mortgages

One of the most perplexing decisions you'll face in buying a home is the choice of a mortgage. Fixed rate mortgages offer security: You will always know the size of your monthly payment. Adjustable rate mortgages give you flexibility and the potential of saving money because the initial rate is lower, but an adjustable rate mortgage carries the risk of much higher payments when interest rates rise. If you want stability, a fixed rate mortgage is for you; if you like to take risks, you'll be attracted to an adjustable mortgage.

Using the Spreadsheet for the Figures That Matter Most

When you first use the mortgage spreadsheet, you should experiment with only the figures in cells B4 through B10, to learn how much you can afford. Later, after you've done more homework, you can adjust the figures in the closing costs section, from cells B13 to B25.

The spreadsheet assumes you'll pay a 10 percent deposit on contract and another 10 percent down payment at the time of closing, which is one of the most typical arrangements. If you plan to pay a different percentage for the down payment, change the equation in cell B10. Cell B10 calculates the contract deposit (the first down payment which is put into escrow until closing) by multiplying the purchase price by ten percent (the formula is =B4*.10). Cell B13 calculates the second down payment which is made at the time of closing. Typically, the initial down payment is mandated by the seller's attorney and ten percent is very standard; the second down payment is negotiated between you and the bank writing your mortgage. Many banks require a minimum of a 20 percent total downpayment, leading to the standard of two ten percent down payments. If you would like the spreadsheet to automatically calculate the size of the mortgage, based on a 20 percent total down payment, you'll find instructions in the spreadsheet in the rows just below the closing costs calculation. It will tell you how to change the entry in the mortgage cell to be 80 percent of the total home purchase.

You may need to tinker with the spreadsheet so it mirrors your situation. For example, your bank may not include taxes in your monthly payment. This spreadsheet does. It's a good idea to include the impact of taxes on your budget, and so you may not want to change the spreadsheet formulas if this applies to you, but you may want to change the labels in cells D1 through D3 to indicate that the mortgage payment is the first calculation, and the next two add the taxes to the monthly payment. The formula in cell E3 simply adds taxes (divided by twelve to reflect monthly payments) to the mortgage payment.

But few of us can clearly say we'll always be a risk-taker or a risk-avoider. Our main goal is to make sure we're getting the best deal, and it's worth taking some effort to make sure you do. The choice between the two types of mortgages will affect your personal finances dramatically: The difference of two percentage points (which is usually the largest gap between the two rates after the first two years) can represent tens of thousands of dollars in cost over the life of the loan.

For most comparisons, the adjustable rate mortgage will remain a better choice for the first three or four years. But after that, the fixed rate mortgage will probably be the better choice, since the adjustable rate mortgage has a higher maximum rate. Many adjustable mortgages are convertible, so you can lock in a rate and change the mortgage to a fixed rate. You may want to use ARM to explore the

➡ The formulas behind the home-buyer's worksheet

This "sum" formula totals the amounts in the two sections below.

The total monthly payment calculates the mortgage payment and then adds the amount paid to escrow for property taxes.

A contract deposit is usually ten percent of the purchase price. For a different percentage you'd change 0.1 to a different figure.

Microsoft Works - [MORTGAGE.WK1]

File   Edit   View   Insert   Format   Tools   Window   Help

Arial   10

E3   =PMT(B5,(B6/12),(B8*12))+E2

	A	B	C	D	E
1	Cash needed to buy a house	=SUM(B27+B10)		Monthly loan payment	=PMT(B5,(B6/12),(B8*12))
2				Monthly escrow (taxes)	=B9/12
3	COST OF HOME & MORTGAGE			Total monthly payment	=PMT(B5,(B6/12),(B8*12))+E2
4	Price of the house	175000	<		
5	Mortgage Amount	140000	<		
6	Mortgage Interest Rate	0.085	<		
7	Points Charged by Lender	2	<		
8	Loan Term	30	<		
9	Annual Real Estate Taxes	4000	<		
10	Contract Deposit	=B4*0.1			
11					
12	CLOSING COSTS				
13	Down payment at closing	=(B4-B5)-B10			
14	Inspection of house	350	<		
15	Mortgage Insurance	650	<		
16	Attorney's fee	4000	<		
17	Loan origination fee	750	<		
18	Recording fee	100	<		
19	Appraisal	300	<		
20	Loan application fee	300	<		
21	Survey	300	<		
22	Title search and insurance	600	<		
23	Homeowner's insurance	1000	<		
24	State and local transfer tax	1500	<		
25	Other costs		<		
26					
27	TOTAL CLOSING COSTS	=SUM(B13:B25)			

Press ALT to choose commands, or F2 to edit.   NUM

➡ *Understanding Mortgage Choices*

ARM is a program that demonstrates the precise difference between a fixed rate mortgage and an adjustable rate mortgage. You'll find a copy of this shareware program on the CD-ROM that comes with this book; you can use the CD-ROM's main menu to copy it to your hard disk. It's a good idea to copy ARM to its own disk directory. ARM must be run from the DOS prompt; if you're running Windows, you'll need to exit. To run ARM, make sure you have switched your DOS path to the same directory where ARM is stored and then type ARM at the DOS prompt.

The program will ask you for the interest rates you're deciding between, both for the adjustable and fixed mortgages. It will ask for other key factors, such as the size of your mortgage, the amount the adjustable rate mortgage can change each year, and the maximum rate. It will then display a report showing how much interest you'll pay under each option, month by month. In the first year, the adjustable mortgage will cost you less in interest payments. The program assumes the worst-case scenario—the adjustable rate mortgage will rise by the maximum possible rate each year. You see a display for one year at a time, showing each month how much money you're spending in interest payments (the program also figures in the amount you would be earning if you kept the savings in an interest-bearing account). This program is provided as shareware; if you use it, you should register the program and pay the author's nominal fee.

effect of locking in a desired rate after two or three years. To do that, use the rate you hope to lock in as the maximum rate for the adjustable mortgage.

Another major factor in a choosing a mortgage is the question of points, up-front payments that will reduce the interest rate paid on a loan. Points should be regarded as pre-paid interest, paid in addition to the monthly interest charges. You can deduct them on your tax return as an interest expense. To the bank, the purpose of points is to make a lower rate more attractive by speeding up the rate at which the bank is paid for the loan.

You can help decide if points are worth exploring in the spreadsheet MORT-GAGE.WK1 discussed earlier in this chapter. You'd simply change the mortgage rates and points to see the impact on your cash requirements and monthly payment. But to see the long-term impact of buying mortgage points you'll need to run another program on this book's CD-ROM, POINTS. This program is very similar to ARM. It's provided as a shareware program; if you continue to use it after you evaluate it, you should register the program and pay the author's nominal fee. The CD-ROM's main menu will copy it to your hard disk; it's a good idea to copy POINTS to its own directory.

When you run POINTS, you'll be asked for details of the loan, including the points being charged and the interest rate of the mortgage. The program will then display a report on how much you'll pay in interest in either scenario. You'll find that a mortgage without points is cheaper for the first couple of years, since the program includes the cost of points in the first month's payment. In most cases, around the third or fourth year, the mortgage with points will be more economical and, over time, it will remain the better choice. The program will show you the exact month in which you'll begin to save by paying points, and then will show how much you'll save from that time forward.

9 Paying for College

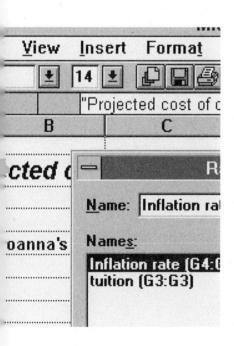

146 Shopping for Colleges

149 Creating a Strategy for Your College Fund

154 A Monthly Savings Plan: How Much Is Enough?

College

costs have grown at such a ferocious rate in recent years that it seems as though they will never stop rising. Many parents hear the frightening news and become scared into inaction: It seems hopeless. However, the situation is far from hopeless. In fact, you may be in better shape than you think. No matter how young your children are, you can benefit from spending a little bit of time to learn about today's college costs. You'll find that you actually have a wide range of choices. For example, while Ivy League schools have hefty bills, many state universities are well within the reach of most families—if you start to save early enough. And while college tuition rose very sharply during the 1980s, costs are now growing at a rate closer to the general inflation rate.

This chapter shows you how to create a strategy for sending children to college. You'll learn the following:

✔ Find accurate information about college costs

✔ Use that information to build a spreadsheet-based savings plan

You'll be able to use this strategy for years, once you understand how to learn about college costs and how to build your own savings plan.

Shopping for Colleges

Your first stop in preparing for college should be to browse through one of the college databases available through the major online services. America Online offers the College Board Handbook (Keyword: College) and CompuServe provides Peterson's College Database (Go Petersons). Both list more than 3,000 schools, for which they provide the essential details, including entrance requirements, degree programs, and background on campus life. The information is comparable to that found in printed books, but you can search through the online database to focus on schools that meet certain criteria—for example, majors offered, locations, and admission difficulty.

Most important for parents, there's cost information, including tuition, fees, and living expenses.

College *is within reach.*

With some planning, you'll have a wide range of choices.

Parents of high-school-age children will want to sit down as a family and review the information. As always, be prepared to save or print the information first, to keep your online costs down. Because colleges can be searched by many variables, in addition to learning about costs, the databases can help you choose a school, too.

After you learn the basics, you'll also learn a little about the financial aid programs available for each school. You won't find out enough to help you figure out if you're eligible, but just enough to give you hope that aid may be there when you need it.

 ### Where to find facts about college costs

You can learn the basics, plus information about financial aid.

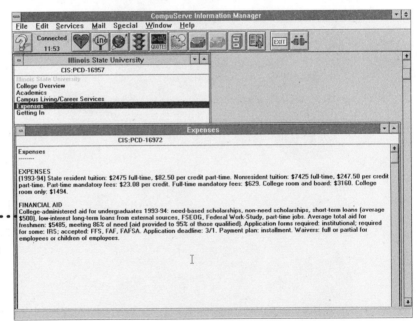

A report from Peterson's College Database on CompuServe

One thing you'll learn from reading financial information on these colleges is that tuition is only one of many expenses. Books, university fees, and living expenses are significant costs.

Even if your children are far from college age, it's worth a quick look at the college costs in these databases to help you start planning, especially if you have strong feelings about the type of school you want your children to attend. The difference in cost between state schools and private schools, for example, is enormous, and you may need to accelerate your savings if you have a particularly expensive school in mind.

Creating a Strategy for Your College Fund

Once you have some idea of how much tuition and room and board cost today, you'll be in a position to project how much it will cost when your children are ready. You'll find a college calculator in Quicken, but it's far from adequate. Many of us need to plan for more than one tuition, and we also need to plan for rising costs—which Quicken doesn't allow.

To create a realistic projection to help in planning to send all of the children in a family to college several years from now, I created a spreadsheet that starts with today's costs and assumes college costs will rise steadily. It's designed to help you decide how much to set aside each month in a savings plan so you'll have enough when the bills arrive. You'll find four files on this book's companion CD-ROM—COLLEGE1.WKS is for families with one child, COLLEGE2.WKS is for families with two children, and so on. In the following pages, we'll explore how the spreadsheets work. When you load the file from disk into your spreadsheet software, you'll find instructions on how to adjust the spreadsheet for the ages of your children.

Predicting the future is an inexact science. In the examples shown here, the inflation rate will certainly fluctuate, and there's no guarantee that college tuition will rise at the same rate as inflation overall. In the 1980s, tuition rose much faster than inflation. But experts maintain that college costs have finished their growth spurt and they're likely to settle down to a predictable rate instead of the spiraling increases we've seen in recent years. If the experts are wrong, you can change the inflation rate in your spreadsheet, but since we have to start somewhere, I've based this projection on 4 percent inflation.

The first goal in our plan is to gain a sense of what college costs will be when your children are ready to go. For the parents of a toddler, that means projecting 15 years or more. And since the spreadsheet will be referred to periodically for years, it makes sense to show the projection for each year so it can be easily adjusted as college choices and prices change. To project college costs, the spreadsheet needs to consider just two variables: the current cost and the inflation rate—everything else will be calculated from these variables.

In this spreadsheet, it makes sense to use range names when we identify factors like tuition and the inflation rate. In earlier chapters, we simply used the addresses of a spreadsheet cell for calculations. Those spreadsheets were designed that way so they'd be easier to understand, but the techniques offer less flexibility. Our college spreadsheet will make repeated use of the same cells, and some families will need to add or delete rows to reflect the age of their children, so we'll want to make it as easy as possible to refer to the cells. Once we've given a name to a range, we no longer need to be concerned about its location; the spreadsheet takes care of it.

➡ A Quick Lesson in Spreadsheet Ranges

A spreadsheet range is one or more cells that have been identified with a name. Once the range is named, you can refer to the cells by using only the name. Ranges can be a big help in building a complex spreadsheet, since you don't need to remember the addresses of cells and your range name can be descriptive of the contents.

A range name should be easy to remember. In the college spreadsheet, the range names identify the purpose of the cell, for example, "inflation rate," and "tuition" identify cells which hold the relevant figures. A range can hold one or many cells, and the contents of the cell can be a value or a formula. To create a range name in Microsoft Works, you first select the cells you want to name. Then, select the Insert menu, and select the Range Name command. Type in a name and press the OK button. You can now refer to the range by its name when you write formulas in other cells.

A spreadsheet range

•••Range name identifies
the contents of this cell•
as "tuition"

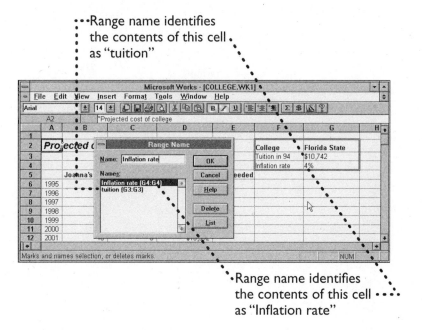

•Range name identifies
the contents of this cell ••••
as "Inflation rate"

Our college-planning spreadsheet starts out with figures found on CompuServe in Peterson's College Database. The tuition (in cell G3) is the total of tuition and living expenses for Florida State University in 1994, a school with costs comparable to other state universities. Just below the tuition is a guess of the inflation rate for the next few years. Both of these cells were identified as ranges, so they can be easily used in the equations that will project college costs over the coming years. When you use the spreadsheet, you'll be able to replace the amount for tuition or inflation as often as you wish.

To build a spreadsheet for a young child, we start by entering the current year and the ages of the children. The spreadsheet saves us the work of filling in numbers for the following years, thanks to the Fill Series command (in Works it's on the Edit menu). It's much easier to use Fill Series than to type in each year and the age of the child that year. To use Fill Series, highlight the first number (either the year or one of the ages) and then move the mouse until you've highlighted a long string of cells. Then select the Fill Series command on the Edit

Projecting the cost of college

Just two variables are needed.

After the spreadsheet is set up, only these values will need to be changed.

		Microsoft Works - [COLLEGE.WK1]						

File Edit View Insert Forma**t** T**o**ols **W**indow **H**elp

Arial   10   **B** *I* U   Σ $

D25   =D24*$Inflation rate+D24

	A	B	C	D	E	F	G	H
1								
2	*Projected cost of college*					College	Florida State	
3				Tuition		Tuition in 94	$10,742	
4				Adjusted for		Inflation rate	4%	
5		Joanna's age	Kate's age	Inflation	Cash needed			
6	1995	4	2	$10,742				
7	1996	5	3	$11,172				
8	1997	6	4	$11,619				
9	1998	7	5	$12,083				
10	1999	8	6	$12,567				
11	2000	9	7	$13,069				
12	2001	10	8	$13,592				
13	2002	11	9	$14,136				
14	2003	12	10	$14,701				
15	2004	13	11	$15,289				
16	2005	14	12	$15,901				
17	2006	15	13	$16,537				
18	2007	16	14	$17,198				
19	2008	17	15	$17,886				
20	2009	18	16	$18,602	$18,602			
21	2010	19	17	$19,346	$19,346			
22	2011	20	18	$20,120	$40,239			
23	2012	21	19	$20,924	$41,849			
24	2013		20	$21,761	$21,761			
25	2014		21	$22,632	$22,632			
26								
27								

Press ALT to choose commands, or F2 to edit.   NUM

The tuition bills likely to be due when the children go to college

menu in Works (in Lotus 1-2-3 and Excel, the fill commands are on the Data menu). The Fill Series dialog box requires you confirm the numbers will increase by one; select OK and the numbers are inserted. For this spreadsheet, we wanted the ages to increase until the girls are 21 and we expect (hope!) the college bills will be finished.

Once we have a structure for the number of years, we use a formula that projects tuition. Those calculations are performed in column D, under the heading "Tuition Adjusted for Inflation." It's easy to see how this was done by looking at

The formulas behind the tuition projection

Formula calculates how
tuition will increase based
on today's inflation rate.

	A	B	C	D	E	F	G
1							
2	**Projec**					College	Florida State
3				Tuition		Tuition in 94	=(6682+4060)
4				Adjusted for		Inflation rate	0.04
5		Joanna's age	Kate's age	Inflation	Cash needed		
6	1995	4	2	=$tuition			
7	1996	5	3	=($tuition+($Inflation rate*$tuition))			
8	1997	6	4	=D7*$Inflation rate+D7			
9	1998	7	5	=D8*$Inflation rate+D8			
10	1999	8	6	=D9*$Inflation rate+D9			
11	2000	9	7	=D10*$Inflation rate+D10			
12	2001	10	8	=D11*$Inflation rate+D11			
13	2002	11	9	=D12*$Inflation rate+D12			
14	2003	12	10	=D13*$Inflation rate+D13			
15	2004	13	11	=D14*$Inflation rate+D14			
16	2005	14	12	=D15*$Inflation rate+D15			
17	2006	15	13	=D16*$Inflation rate+D16			
18	2007	16	14	=D17*$Inflation rate+D17			
19	2008	17	15	=D18*$Inflation rate+D18			
20	2009	18	16	=D19*$Inflation rate+D19	=D20*1		
21	2010	19	17	=D20*$Inflation rate+D20	=D21		
22	2011	20	18	=D21*$Inflation rate+D21	=D22*2		
23	2012	21	19	=D22*$Inflation rate+D22	=D23*2		
24	2013		20	=D23*$Inflation rate+D23	=D24		
25	2014		21	=D24*$Inflation rate+D24	=D25		
26							
27							

Microsoft Works - [COLLEGE.WK1]

File Edit View Insert Format Tools Window Help

Arial   14

A2   "Projected cost of college

Press ALT to choose commands, or F2 to edit.   NUM

The formula that calculates the
cash needed multiplies tuition
by two if both are in school.

the formulas in the spreadsheet display. The logic is very simple. The projection
begins with the tuition in the first year. In later years, we need to take the tuition
and increase it by the amount of inflation. To do this, we multiply the previous
year's tuition by the inflation rate to determine the amount of the increase, and
add that number to the previous year's tuition. Setting up this spreadsheet is not
as tedious as it sounds because after the formula is entered, we can copy it to
every cell where it needs to go.

A Monthly Savings Plan: How Much Is Enough?

The spreadsheet we've built so far has taken us halfway: We have an idea of what tuition will cost when the children are ready. Now we can use that information to build our savings plan.

 Calculating how much to save each month

Tuition is copied.

Only these numbers need to be changed.

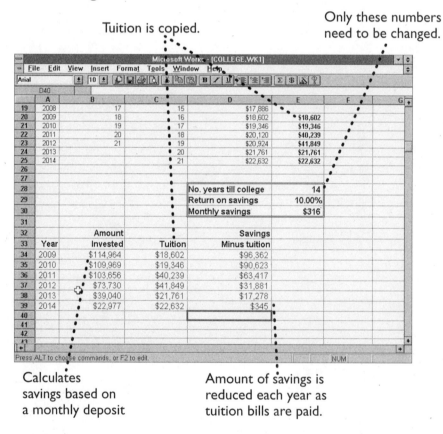

Calculates savings based on a monthly deposit

Amount of savings is reduced each year as tuition bills are paid.

We'll use the projected tuition bill to create our savings plan, so the cells where tuition is shown were copied to a new section of the spreadsheet and identified as Tuition. In this section, the projected tuition will be used to set a target for our savings plan. The tuition will also represent withdrawals from our college fund in the years when we're paying the bills.

Now we have to apply hard math. We want to project the return on our investments over the years, and we want to keep on projecting it during the college years, when we'll be withdrawing money. We wouldn't want to forget the effect of compounded interest during college years, since the fund should be quite large by then and the power of compounding will really be kicking in with strong earnings. The first formula in the "amount invested" column (cell B34) calculates the earnings on fourteen years of savings at 10 percent interest. You'll want to experiment with the values in the spreadsheet for the return on investment. No investment guarantees 10 percent return, but I chose this amount because it's the historical return from investing in the stock market. This plan is created for a family where the child is a toddler, so it's safe to invest in the stock market. When the plan is adjusted for a family with a teenager, the money should be moved to safer investments with lower returns, following the advice outlined in Chapter 4, "Choosing a Fund Strategy."

Once we set up the total our savings will generate and the cost of the tuition, we have to account for the withdrawals each year from the fund for tuition bills. The calculations for the following years need to do two things: calculate the interest earned on the fund after tuition is paid and calculate the growth in the fund from continued installments from our monthly savings plan.

The technique used to calculate the amount in the savings plan is a spreadsheet formula called Future Value (FV). This formula does all of the hard work, using the values you'll enter for the number of years until college, the earnings you expect your savings to provide (for example, 10 percent), and the amount you need to save each month. This last value is the one you will experiment with after you've entered the correct number of years and a percentage that reflects your investment strategy.

To learn how you much you need to save, try different numbers in the monthly savings cell until the last figure under "savings minus tuition" is as close to zero as you can get it. In our sample, $316 was the lowest number we could enter in monthly savings and still have something left after all the tuition bills are paid in the year 2014. A higher amount of monthly savings would give us a larger surplus. A lower amount would produce a shortfall in the last year.

→ **The formulas behind the monthly savings calculation**

Future Value formula calculates the amount the savings plan will earn.

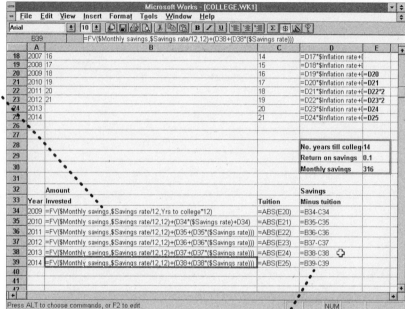

Each year the tuition must be subtracted from the savings fund.

Clearly, the spreadsheet can't predict how much you should save to the penny. We've made a lot of assumptions and we'll be lucky if only half of them are correct. But you're better off working on a plan that you understand than you are making guesses. The value of this plan is that you can adjust it each year to make it more realistic. By the time the children are starting college, it can become the basis of your tuition payment schedule.

10

Saving *Time* and **Money** on Your **Taxes**

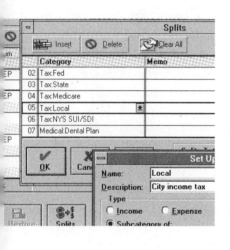

160 How to Get Ahead of the Tax Game

164 How to Get Quicken to Track Tax Expenses

168 Working Smarter in TurboTax

Paying

taxes is not the most pleasant chore, but you want to do the best job you can. Money is at stake. The more you know about deductions and credits, the more you'll save. And if you can do the job yourself, you'll save the cost of paying a professional to complete the forms for you. Of all the financial exercises this book covers, preparing your taxes with software is probably one of the most valuable. You'll find the process is relatively easy and the knowledge you gain is invaluable. A proper understanding of how income taxes affect your personal finance is essential to smart financial planning.

While a good tax program can speed you through the process of preparing your annual 1040 form and the other necessary paperwork, you can also benefit from using the time you gain to better understand how the tax laws affect your finances. The rules change each year, and most Americans fail to claim deductions to which they're entitled. The deductions you may miss range from day care expenses to the cost of tax preparation; and if you can spend a little extra time with your tax software, you may learn enough to save some money on this return and next year's. By experimenting with different values for incomes and deductions, you'll gain perspective on your financial picture that can help you make better financial decisions in the future.

This chapter will help you prepare your records so you'll be efficient in preparing your return. It will also show you how to make the process of completing your return as rewarding as possible. So you pay only what you owe and no more and gain valuable insight into your financial picture.

How to Get Ahead of the Tax Game

There are about a half dozen programs on the market to help individuals prepare their own taxes. All of them are easy to use, and all of them will complete the forms you need to file. If you are using Quicken already, you'll save much more time if you use TurboTax from ChipSoft. These two programs are so closely linked that if you have taken a few small steps in your Quicken accounts, you'll find much of your tax return is prepared almost instantly when you install

---

➡ *Make tax time easier on yourself*

TurboTax. Time that you used to spend looking up numbers and calculating subtotals can be put to better use. TurboTax is also an excellent program in its own right, providing detailed help and an easy-to-learn interface, so no matter which software you use to track your finances, TurboTax is your best choice for preparing your taxes.

If you have been managing your finances in Quicken and following a few simple techniques, you'll find that TurboTax will save you a significant amount of time when you sit down to prepare your annual return because TurboTax can import your Quicken files, filling out much of the form automatically.

Long before you're ready to do your taxes, Quicken can give you an overview of your tax situation. If you select the Tax Planner option on Quicken's Plan menu you'll see a presentation of all the key figures in your tax situation.

When you first open the Tax Planner, no amounts are shown. If you click on the Quicken data button, the program will read through your Quicken data files

Quicken's Tax Planner shows where you stand with the government.

Quicken uses real figures from your checkbook and investment registers to give you a tax overview.

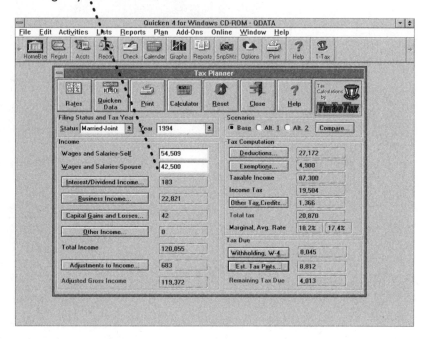

and use your current account information to project your tax situation. You'll have the option of going through the list of tax-related items and telling Quicken whether or not each item should be annualized. Pay attention to these selections because they'll have an impact on the accuracy of the projection. The software makes its best guess on whether the category contains items that recur regularly or are likely to be one-time charges. For example, mortgage interest is usually paid monthly, so Quicken will assume you want to annualize the amounts. If you perform the calculation at the end of September, Quicken will assume 9 out of 12 payments were made already, so the yearly amount should be 33 percent higher than the current total. On the other hand, capital gains distributions tend to be one-time payments, so Quicken would not annualize these.

If your income is based on paychecks, your tax situation may not change much during the course of the year, and the tax planner will be able to give you a fairly accurate view ahead of time of what you'll have to pay (or get back). You can use this information to your advantage even if your financial dealings are relatively simple. If the Tax Planner estimates you'll be due for a large refund, you may want to change the number of exemptions in order to increase your payroll withholding. While it's nice to have a big refund in the spring, a big refund really means the government is holding money you should be receiving when you're paid. For pay earned early in the year, that means the government is holding your money for over a year without interest. To adjust the number of exemptions used by your employer to calculate your withholding tax, contact your employer's payroll office and complete a new W-4 form; you can claim a higher number of exemptions for withholding purposes than you are allowed on your federal return, so don't feel constrained by the number of exemptions you'll claim on the 1040 form. (The instructions on the W-4 form are quite complex; for help, you can use TurboTax's W-4 estimator.)

If your income fluctuates during the course of the year, you can use Quicken's Tax Planner to get a fair estimate of your tax liability, and you can also play "what-if" games with Tax Planner, changing key figures like income and business expenses. The software lets you compare your actual figures with two alternate scenarios. If you're self-employed, you'll need to pay special attention to the way Quicken calculates annualized amounts, and you'll also want to experiment with the alternate scenarios.

The final factor on whether Tax Planner's estimates are accurate lies with the U.S. Congress: If major changes are made to the tax code during the year, Quicken's estimate will be out of date. But if Congress enacts only minor changes, you should find Tax Planner to be a fairly good indicator of how much Uncle Sam wants from you.

How to Get Quicken to Track Tax Expenses

When you install Quicken, the program sets up links between income and expense categories that are typical of most households and the IRS's tax forms. For example, interest income is linked with Schedule B if it's above $400 or linked with Form 1040 if it's below $400. You benefit from these links in three ways.

➔ Quicken's tax planner uses real data to project your tax situation.

➔ Quicken can generate a tax summary showing all of your tax-related expenses.

➔ Quicken can export the data to the right forms if you use TurboTax to prepare your tax return.

Quicken has set up some of these categories automatically—for example, a check that was assigned to Charity would be automatically linked with the line on Schedule A where charitable donations are listed—but you must take the time to assign your income and expenses to the correct categories.

Many personal transactions are not tracked as readily as the above example, and you may have to put in some extra effort if you want to have an accurate view of your tax situation. For example, most salary checks include about a half-dozen tax categories that are identical from one pay period to the next. If you use Quicken's Splits tool to identify each of these categories, such as Social Security tax, federal tax, and local tax, you'll be ahead of the game when you start to prepare your taxes, because TurboTax will read the Quicken categories and insert both categories on the correct line.

TIP

If you've been using Quicken and have not been assigning categories to entries in your check register, you should set up your transactions the next time you pay bills. You may find it's worthwhile to go back and change the category designations for older transactions, too, but don't spend too much time on this job. The main value of setting up categories for tax-related items is to save time when you prepare your tax return. You'll only save time if you're capturing the data as you go along, and that happens if you set up memorized transactions to use over and over again. If you go back through old transactions and reassign payments, you may be investing more time than you can save. Of course, if you're self-employed and you need to accurately predict your tax situation so you can prepare quarterly tax projections, you'll probably find the time spent adjusting your transactions is time well spent.

➔ Common Tax-Related Transactions

Here are some of the categories that Quicken will set up automatically:

- ➔ Charitable donations
- ➔ Child care payments
- ➔ Interest earned on bank accounts
- ➔ Interest from investments
- ➔ Medical expenses
- ➔ Mortgage payments
- ➔ Salary checks

Quicken can give you an accurate projection of your tax liability and can transfer tax-related payments to the correct tax form on TurboTax if you assigned them correctly when you recorded the transaction.

If you're eager to get an estimate of your tax liability and you're willing to invest the time, the first step is to examine the list of categories used to identify income and expenses. You'll find the list when you select Categories & Transfers from the Lists menu. Categories that are linked with a tax form are clearly identified with the word *tax*. If you want to see which form Quicken uses, click on the category name and select the Edit tool. If you find an item that should be linked with a tax form—especially categories you created—use the Edit tool to assign the category to the right tax form.

The next step is to make sure all of your transactions are being assigned to the correct category. After you've become familiar with the categories and learned which affect your taxes, look through items in your register and double-check them for accuracy. You may find you've set up a special category for expenses that you now realize are tax deductible. Perhaps you set up a new category for checks written to your church. You don't need to change the category assignments if all of the payments are correctly entered; instead, you can link the category with the tax form. Your church category can be edited so there is a link with Schedule A. These transactions will now be added to any other categories under Charity.

Many tax-related expenses are buried inside larger payments. A typical paycheck includes federal, state, and Social Security taxes. In addition, you may be making contributions to tax-exempt retirement accounts, such as IRAs and 401k plans. You'll want to make sure you use the Splits command to allocate every item on your paycheck to the correct category. Start the split item with the gross pay and then enter each deduction as a negative amount. Be sure you select categories that are linked with tax forms (you can see the details for each category by selecting Category & Transfer from Quicken's List menu). For basic categories such as federal tax, you can rely on Quicken's default categories, but you will probably need to add some new categories for situations unique to you. City taxes, for example, need to be entered as a new tax category that will be linked with the line on the W2 form for local withholding taxes.

➔ Early Start or False Start?

Don't be too eager to get started with your taxes. Every year, tax software arrives in stores right after Thanksgiving, even though most of us don't receive the official W-4 and 1099 forms we'll need until late January. These "head start" versions cannot be used to file your return; they have most of the features needed to complete your return, but not all. You'll receive a coupon good for the final program when it's ready.

These software packages are gobbled up by people who are eager to get a big refund or who have some end-of-year decisions to make that will affect their tax liability. If all you want to do is spend as little time as possible doing taxes, then be patient and wait for the next version of the software to ship. You'll only have to install the software once—not twice. The final version should be on sale in late January—just around the time you'll be receiving your tax income statements from financial institutions and employers. But don't wait until the last minute. Tax software sells fast in early April and stores run out.

Mortgage payments also include tax-deductible payments, but because a typical mortgage payment is based on a different interest payment each month, you need to handle them in a special way. A typical mortgage payment includes three distinct payments: interest, a portion of the loan principal, and property taxes, usually identified as escrow (some mortgage payments also include installments on homeowner's insurance as part of the escrow account). Because mortgage payments use a sliding scale to ensure that interest is paid at a higher rate than the principal, you need to calculate the division between interest and principal in each payment.

TurboTax gets a head start when Quicken categories are properly set up.

TurboTax reads in items from a Quicken checkbook that are relevant to your tax return.

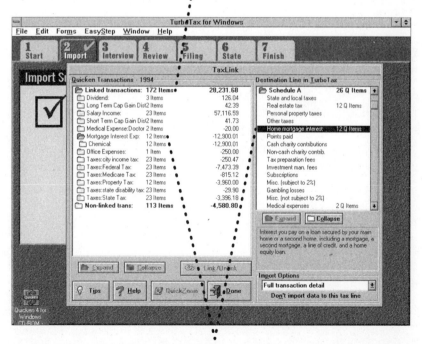

Monthly payments of mortgage interest are linked to Schedule A on the correct line.

The first payments on a mortgage are composed almost entirely of interest; with each payment to follow, the amount of interest paid decreases and the amount of principal increases. In order to properly allocate a mortgage payment with Quicken, you need to set up the transaction as a loan payment; Quicken will correctly divide your payments into interest and principal, assigning the interest to a tax-deductible category. When you set up your mortgage transaction, make sure you have your mortgage payment book or a statement at hand. Then, select Loans on Quicken's Activities menu and enter the details of your loan. You'll have a choice of paying the mortgage automatically as a scheduled transaction or adding it to the list of your payments as a memorized transaction. Either way, Quicken will correctly allocate each payment of mortgage interest as a tax-deductible item.

Working Smarter in TurboTax

If you've prepared your Quicken files for TurboTax, the process of completing your form will be measured in minutes rather than hours. Once you import data from Quicken to TurboTax, you can sit back and answer questions in the program's Interview module; if the data is at your fingertips, you'll be able to finish your return in one sitting.

TurboTax gives you the option of completing the forms on your own, but only tax professionals will want to. Most of us will be better off using the Interview, which takes us through the process of completing the return by asking questions. All you need to do is supply the answers; if a category of forms doesn't apply to you, the Interview spares you from answering many questions. But if your situation has tax implications, such as owning a home, the Interview will probe you for details and prod you to claim all possible deductions. If you don't understand the question, click on the underlined terms; a window will open with an explanation.

TIP

Don't be too hasty and assume that the software has done all of the work accurately. The import procedure does have flaws, so you need to check your figures. And some of the assumptions you made in Quicken may be distorted when imported into TurboTax. Childcare expenses, for example, are tax-deductible only if

TurboTax offers help at every turn.

Turbo Tax can guide you through each form, one step at a time.

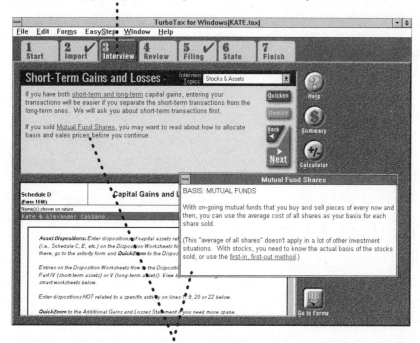

You can see an explanation of key terms by clicking on underlined phrases.

the facility is properly certified; if you've been classifying your payments to an un-certified facility through Quicken, they will be entered on a tax form in TurboTax. It's your responsibility to make sure the entire form is properly filled out and that you are legally entitled to the deduction.

Interest payments, withholding tax, and divided payments should all be cross-checked against statements you receive in the mail. Most important is a "re-ality check." Do the figures look right? The software guides you through the pro-cess so quickly that you may make a mistake, too. Remember that if the return is audited, you'll have to justify your deductions by yourself. No one from the soft-ware company will be there to explain them.

TurboTax seems so thorough and intelligent that you may be lulled into accepting all of its advice too quickly. The program comes with many explanations of terms, but you have to take the initiative and read through any topic you don't understand thoroughly.

➔ Where to Find Help

Tax preparation programs have built-in help systems, but they can't answer all of your questions.

Many people find they can get some help by reading through the messages on one of the online personal finance discussion groups, especially in the months leading up to April 15. Every online service has at least one finance area. One of the better places to look is the bulletin board maintained by the maker of your tax software. On CompuServe, type GO CHIPSOFT to find discussions about TurboTax. You'll find separate areas for discussion of the program and tax issues.

If you rely on advice obtained through a discussion group, remember that you're the one who'll be held responsible if there's a mistake. An accountant hired to prepare your return is legally responsible for the return; a stranger who gives you advice on an online service could be a nut who likes to cause trouble.

The least expensive way to get tax help is from the IRS. A number of studies have shown that the IRS does not always provide accurate answers, but the same can be said of any professional. When calling the IRS, be prepared for a long wait—have reading material on hand and call from a speaker phone if possible so you won't have to hold the receiver to your ear. You could be on hold for ten minutes or more. The number is 800-829-1040.

Once you've completed the forms, be sure to take advantage of three review options. TurboTax will examine your return, looking for obvious errors and possible savings. The software's review can look for deductions and alert you to the possibility of claiming them if you haven't already. For example, if you've registered a car you may be able to deduct your automobile registration fees as a personal property tax; if TurboTax doesn't see the deduction listed, it will point this out.

Have you claimed every deduction the IRS allows?

Turbo Tax will look for statements likely to trigger an IRS audit on your return.

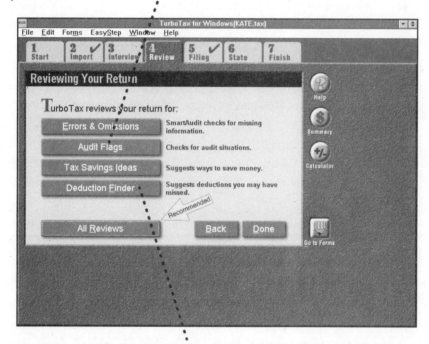

The software can help you learn about deductions you didn't know about.

If you have a complex tax situation, you may encounter situations you don't understand, despite all of the help available to you. While TurboTax may help you learn enough about the tax code to make sure you're doing a good job, if you're not completely confident, be sure to consult an accountant. The money spent on TurboTax won't be lost because you're certain to be better organized as a result of using the program and you should be spending less on accounting advice. In fact, many accountants use TurboTax to crunch the numbers, so you may find your accountant will be able to use your files, saving time for both of you.

→ Keeping Good Records

How long should you save your tax software and data files? Tax laws say the IRS can take up to three years to audit your return, and an additional three years to audit if there's suspicion that income was underreported by more than 25 percent. So you should keep for six years any records that support your position in a fight with the IRS.

In preparing your tax return, you probably made notes explaining what some of the income and deductions represent, so in most cases, you'll want to keep the software and the data files. You will want to free up the disk space the tax software uses after you've prepared your return, so you should copy the data files onto a floppy disk and store the floppy disk with the original program disks and manuals. It's a good idea to be cautious. After you've copied the data files onto a floppy, run the tax software and try to open the data files on the floppy. If the tax software can read the floppy disk files, you've got a good copy. If it can't, try again; you may have copied the wrong file.

After you're sure the floppy has the right files, you can delete from your hard disk the data files, the tax software program files, and the directory where the program was installed. If you use TurboTax, use the program's un-install option; it's easier than deleting the files. Store the software and data along with the paper records of your return.

As you complete your return, you don't need to have actual receipts for de-ductions, such as business expenses and charitable contributions. You can create your return by reading through your checkbook register or by im-porting Quicken files. But if you're audited, the IRS will want something more concrete than your records. It will want to see receipts showing the amounts and details of each transaction. Canceled checks may be sufficient for some transactions but not others. For example, charitable donations can be substantiated with a canceled check only for donations up to $250. Donations above $250 require written proof from the charitable institution. You should keep along with the software every single bill and receipt for transactions that can be claimed as tax deductions.

TurboTax, like most tax programs, allows you to file your return electronically. The option is attractive if you're expecting a refund, but don't expect to see the check zipped back at the same speed you sent it off. Electronic filing also requires that you complete a form, sign it, and mail it. The IRS waits until an intermediary service bureau processes the paperwork before it releases a check. Electronic filing may reduce the time you wait for your refund from as long as ten weeks to as little as two weeks, but there's no guarantee. And if you're paying taxes instead of receiving a refund, you don't gain anything by speeding through your return.

Retirement projection
Accumulated funds 1953-1998

SDI ....
IRA ....
Investments......
  Stocks..........
  Bonds..........
Interest ....

Retirement fund

11 Planning for Retirement

	A	B	C	D	E
1	**Projecting the value of today's retirement s:**				
2		Annual contribution	$12,000		
3		Interest on ann cont.	10%		
4		Retirement age	65	You'll have	$1,418,7:
5		Current age	45		
6					
7		IRA	IRA	401-K	401-K
8	Age	Account	Rate	Account	Rate
9			10.0%		9.0%
10					
11	45	$10,000		$25,000	
12	46	$11,000		$27,250	
13	47	$12,100		$29,703	
14	48	$13,310		$32,376	
15	49	$14,641		$35,290	
16	50	$16,105		$38,466	
17	51	$17,716		$41,928	
18	52	$19,487		$45,701	
19	53	$21,436		$49,814	
20	54	$23,579		$54,297	
21	55	$25,937		$59,184	
22	56	$28,531		$64,511	

176 How Much Income Will You Need?

181 Projecting the Growth of Your Savings

185 How Long Will Your Savings Last?

188 Getting the Most from Your Savings

Planning

for retirement has never been more essential. Over the last few decades, millions of Americans retired on comfortable pensions, promised to them by their employers as rewards for loyal service and delivered on schedule, with a guarantee the monthly checks would continue for life. Today, few workers can look forward to such a secure future. The benefit plans that provided guaranteed payments in the past are being phased out in favor of contribution plans that promise only to set aside some money and to invest it on behalf of the employee. No monthly checks are promised, and for many of us, the amount that will be available when we retire may be far less than we need. For many Americans, a comfortable retirement will require savings far in excess of a million dollars.

Don't make the mistake of waiting until it's too late to start planning your retirement income. Your best ally is time; money set aside at an early age will grow considerably. Even if you believe you have a generous company retirement plan, you should be looking at the numbers with a view toward making it last through retirement. We all face uncertainty in attempting to plan 10 or 20 or 30 years from now, but we can make some reasonable assumptions that will help ensure the best retirement possible.

In this chapter, you'll learn how to project your needs and the growth of your retirement savings using simple spreadsheets. We'll then put those two together to create a retirement budget that will tell you if your current savings are sufficient and, if not, how much you'll need to put aside.

How Much Income Will You Need?

The first step in making an adequate plan for retirement is to make an assumption about how much you'll need. Inflation is certain to continue, so today's income figures aren't a good guide until you project the impact of steady inflation. Even if inflation stays at a relatively modest 4 percent, the effect will be jarring. For example, someone who earns $75,000 today will probably need to earn $208,000 25 years from now to maintain the same standard of living.

Rather than pick numbers out of thin air, we can use a spreadsheet to help us project exactly how inflation will affect today's salaries to get an idea of what a

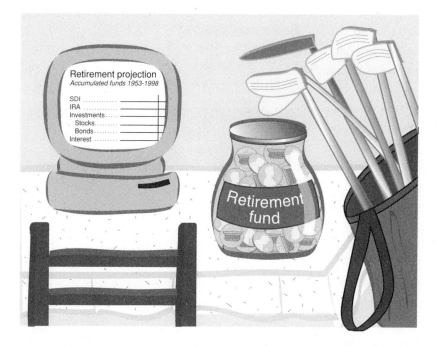

→ Don't let retirement sneak up on you!

Using a few simple spreadsheets on your computer, you can determine how much you'll need to save each year to assure a comfortable retirement.

comfortable income will be when we reach retirement age. Then, we can make a few assumptions about social security to get a realistic idea of the income we should plan to have.

You can run the spreadsheet RET_NEED.WKS by copying it from this book's CD-ROM to your computer and opening it with either Microsoft Works, Lotus 1-2-3, or Microsoft Excel. You'll find it in the directory \CHAPTER.11 under Worksheets along with the other spreadsheet used in this chapter.

When you run the spreadsheet, you can explore your options by changing the values that appear inside the box at the top of the spreadsheet. First, you should pick the income level, based on today's salaries, at which you'd like to retire. People in their twenties, thirties, and forties will want to pick a salary higher

Project your retirement income.

The RET_NEED.WKS spreadsheet (included on the CD) lets you take inflation into account in projecting the income you'll need to retire. Note that inflation will have a big impact on earnings.

Retirement income is found in the table at right and adjusted downward by 20%.

Current income is increased at the inflation rate.

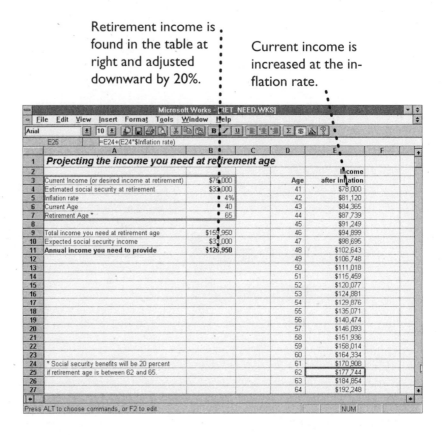

Microsoft Works - [RET_NEED.WKS]

File Edit View Insert Format Tools Window Help

Arial

E25   =E24+(E24*Inflation rate)

	A	B	C	D	E	F
1	*Projecting the income you need at retirement age*					
2					Income	
3	Current Income (or desired income at retirement)	$75,000		Age	after inflation	
4	Estimated social security at retirement	$30,000		41	$78,000	
5	Inflation rate	4%		42	$81,120	
6	Current Age	40		43	$84,365	
7	Retirement Age *	65		44	$87,739	
8				45	$91,249	
9	Total income you need at retirement age	$159,950		46	$94,899	
10	Expected social security income	$33,000		47	$98,695	
11	**Annual income you need to provide**	**$126,950**		48	$102,643	
12				49	$106,748	
13				50	$111,018	
14				51	$115,459	
15				52	$120,077	
16				53	$124,881	
17				54	$129,876	
18				55	$135,071	
19				56	$140,474	
20				57	$146,093	
21				58	$151,936	
22				59	$158,014	
23				60	$164,334	
24	* Social security benefits will be 20 percent			61	$170,908	
25	if retirement age is between 62 and 65.			62	$177,744	
26				63	$184,854	
27				64	$192,248	

Press ALT to choose commands, or F2 to edit.   NUM

than today's earnings. If you're closer to retirement age, you may be happy to base your retirement income on your current salary or even a bit lower.

Some experts advise you to project your salary at retirement age by increasing today's by 5 percent a year and then adding the effect of inflation. I believe this is unrealistic and likely to make retirement planning seem like an unmanageable burden. In our example, someone with a current salary of $75,000 today would plan to retire on over $500,000—that may be a nice dream, but unless you have a secret source of funds, it's more of a discouragement than a help. This spreadsheet will let you experiment so you can try to pick a salary level that seems reasonable.

The spreadsheet will calculate the impact of inflation based on the income figure you choose.

The spreadsheet will calculate the impact of inflation based on the income figure you choose. If inflation changes from today's 4 percent, you can adjust that number and the future salaries will be adjusted. This spreadsheet generates salary figures based on the impact of inflation for the next 40 years; it displays the salary figures on a line next to a series of ages, starting with your current age. Then, it will look up the salary based on the age you plan to retire. In our spreadsheet, a VLOOKUP formula searches through the list of salaries to find the inflation-adjusted income at retirement age. The lookup formula is set up so it will look for the retirement age you entered and it will provide your retirement income in the cell immediately to the right.

Rather than use the income level at your retirement age, the spreadsheet adjusts the figure downward by 20 percent to reflect the advice of most retirement planners. This downward adjustment is based on the fact that many of the day-to-day bills you face now will be gone when you retire. For example, ideally your house will be paid off, the children will be finished with school, and you'll no longer have job-related expenses.

Once you have a realistic idea of the income you want to have, you'll be able to start looking at your ability to supply the money. But before you calculate the value of your pension plans, consider one outside factor: social security. While you don't want to retire solely on social security, you can make a reasonable assumption that it will be there to supplement your income. In fact, you can even receive a written estimate from the government of the amount you can expect. Social security payments are based on the level of contributions you make while you're working, so it's impossible to generalize. Our projection was based on taking today's average benefits for a married couple and projecting it at 4 percent inflation. It is a very good idea to ask for the government's estimate, partly to help in your planning and partly because you may be able to correct errors in the estimate. Your benefits are calculated from your income, based on government records. When you ask for an estimate of benefits, you also see the recent income statements; if they're wrong, you can have them amended. The form you need to complete is SSA-7004; you can request it by calling the Social Security Administration at 800-772-1213.

The formulas behind the retirement income projections

Ages are calculated on the value entered in B6.

	Microsoft Works - [RET_NEED.WKS]			
File Edit View Insert Format Tools Window Help				
Arial 10				
B9 =VLOOKUP(Retirement Age,D4:E64,1)*0.8				
	A	B	D	E
1	*Projecting the income y*			
2				Income
3	Current Income (or desired income at re	75000	Age	after inflation
4	Estimated social security at retirement	33000	=Current Age+1	=Current Income+(Current I
5	Inflation rate	0.04	=D4+1	=E4+(E4*$Inflation rate)
6	Current Age	40	=D5+1	=E5+(E5*$Inflation rate)
7	Retirement Age *	65	=D6+1	=E6+(E6*$Inflation rate)
8			=D7+1	=E7+(E7*$Inflation rate)
9	Total income you need at retirement age	=VLOOKUP(Retirement Age,D4:E64,1)*0.8	=D8+1	=E8+(E8*$Inflation rate)
10	Expected social security income	=Social security	=D9+1	=E9+(E9*$Inflation rate)
11	**Annual income you need to provide**	=B9-B10	=D10+1	=E10+(E10*$Inflation rate)
12			=D11+1	=E11+(E11*$Inflation rate)
13			=D12+1	=E12+(E12*$Inflation rate)
14			=D13+1	=E13+(E13*$Inflation rate)
15		Range Name	=D14+1	=E14+(E14*$Inflation rate)
16			=D15+1	=E15+(E15*$Inflation rate)
17		Name: Current Income OK	=D16+1	=E16+(E16*$Inflation rate)
18			=D17+1	=E17+(E17*$Inflation rate)
19		Names: Cancel	=D18+1	=E18+(E18*$Inflation rate)
20		Current Age (B6:B6)	=D19+1	=E19+(E19*$Inflation rate)
21		Current Income (B3:B3) Help	=D20+1	=E20+(E20*$Inflation rate)
22		Inflation rate (B5:B5)	=D21+1	=E21+(E21*$Inflation rate)
23		Retirement Age (B7:B7) Delete	=D22+1	=E22+(E22*$Inflation rate)
24		Social security (B4:B4)	=D23+1	=E23+(E23*$Inflation rate)
25	if	List	=D24+1	=E24+(E24*$Inflation rate)
26			=D25+1	=E25+(E25*$Inflation rate)
27			=D26+1	=E26+(E26*$Inflation rate)
Marks and names selection, or deletes marks				NUM

VLOOKUP formula finds the desired retirement age from the age-income table and returns the income value at the correct age.

We want to treat social security benefits as a fixed amount because even though the government will determine your benefit by looking at your income, you have little control over the amount you'll receive. The rules governing social security are likely to change repeatedly over the years, but you should keep in mind that retirement benefits are paid in full at age 65; you can retire at age 62, 63, or 64, but your benefits will be 20 percent lower and they'll stay lower for the rest of your life.

Now that you have some idea of what you'll need each year to retire in comfort, let's see how to get there.

Projecting the Growth of Your Savings

If you haven't already built up a substantial amount of savings and investments for retirement—either on your own or through a company plan—the next few pages will convince you of how urgent it is to start right away. Let's say you would like to follow the scenario in the previous section. You're 35 years old and would like to retire at age 65 with an income equivalent to $75,000 today: You'll need $2.7 million by the time you're 65. If you've got $200,000 put away right now, you can sit back and relax; otherwise, you better start saving.

Procrastination can be very painful. A 40-year-old who wanted to retire at the same age and the same income would need to have $250,000 set aside today. Few of us have anywhere near that amount available. Instead, we have to look at all of our savings and then try to set aside as much as we can every month. Deciding how much to set aside is not easy.

One of the best ways to prepare yourself is to create spreadsheets that you can use over the years to accurately reflect what you've already set aside. Once you know how much you'll need, you can look at where you are today. The next spreadsheet we'll build is titled RET_SAV.WKS; it's also in the \CHAPTER.11 directory of the CD-ROM under Worksheets.

The spreadsheet is designed to track several accounts and estimate how long the money will last during retirement. Most of us are investing retirement money in a variety of ways, including mutual fund accounts, IRAs, Keogh plans, and company retirement plans. We're also making plans for annual contributions in

A savings plan for retirement

Use this spreadsheet to track your savings accounts and estimate how long your retirement money will last.

Amounts entered in boxes are used to calculate the growth of savings acounts.

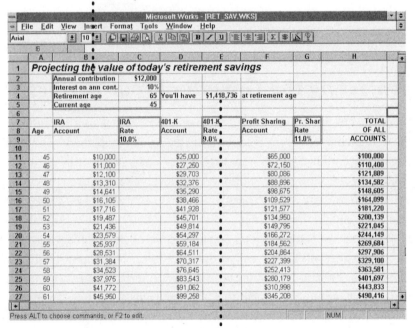

Total of current savings accounts projected until retirement age and annual contributions made from this year until retirement

addition to what's been saved already. You can make better decisions if you create a spreadsheet with realistic numbers that you can use to explore your options in the coming years.

The spreadsheet starts with your savings today and projects the growth of the savings to give you a year-by-year summary of your plan. These projections comprise the series of numbers you see. In addition, the spreadsheet calculates separately the value of annual contributions you'll make so you can adjust your savings plans to help you reach your goal.

You can start to use the spreadsheet right away to learn how your current retirement savings will grow. All you need to know is how much you have socked away right now and a rough idea of the growth rates for these accounts. Then, you can keep on using it year by year with the actual numbers from these accounts. Each year, you should replace the formulas that calculate the values of your IRA, 401k, and profit-sharing account with the actual numbers. The spreadsheet will automatically adjust its calculations to reflect your current holdings.

While the spreadsheet is simple to use and you may never need to adjust it, you'll benefit from understanding how it works so you can create your own variations. At the top of the spreadsheet are boxes where you'll enter personal information, such as your age, the age you'd like to retire, and the amount you've already saved. The spreadsheet then projects how each account will grow each year, based on the interest rates you've entered for each account.

All of these variables are used by formulas that perform the calculations. For example, in cell E4, a future value (FV) formula determines the number of years your savings will earn interest by subtracting current age from retirement age. The spreadsheet also uses the two ages to build the table where your current savings are projected from today into the future.

The total amount you'll have at retirement, shown in cell E4, is calculated by combining two numbers: the total of savings when you reach retirement age, and the future value of the money you plan to add as an annual contribution. The spreadsheet finds the total value of your savings using a VLOOKUP formula that searches through the table where total savings are projected to find the age you plan to retire; then it finds the amount of savings stored seven cells to the right. The spreadsheet calculates the value of your annual contribution using a future value formula that projects the value of an investment based on constant installments. The formula uses the interest rate you enter just below the value for annual contribution, and it calculates the number of years by subtracting your current age from your retirement age.

The formulas behind the retirement savings plan

The formula in cell E4 looks up the total for savings at Retirement Age and adds it to the future value of annual contributions.

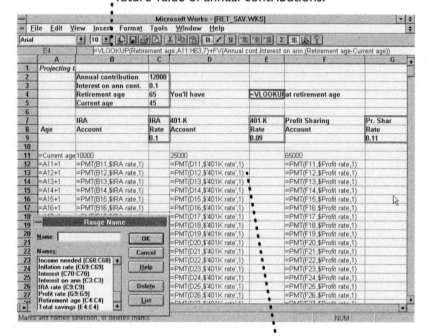

Value of savings is projected after the first year but values can be changed in subsequent years to reflect actual growth.

The spreadsheet was created with just three accounts to make it easy to understand and view. Over time, you'll probably end up with more than three accounts. You can add them in two ways. The most complete solution is to insert two new columns for each account; one column will hold the interest rate and the second the amount. You can copy the formulas for the previous accounts into your new columns; the spreadsheet will automatically adjust the names of the cells. You will need to manually change the formula in the Total of All Accounts column to include the new cells. For example, the cell in H11 should be changed from =SUM(B11:F11) to =SUM(B11:H11). Once you change the first cell in the column, you can copy it into all of the cells below and the spreadsheet will adjust the values.

How Long Will Your Savings Last?

Now that we've seen how easy it is to build huge sums (on paper anyway), we need to see how long the retirement fund will last. Further down in the same spreadsheet, you can work on a balance sheet that will use the amount you've saved at the time of retirement and build a table showing the effect of regular withdrawals. To get an accurate picture, you need to account for the continuing effect of inflation. And you need to include the continuing growth of your savings.

This spreadsheet also lets you experiment with different values to enter in the box in the section "Projecting cash flow in the retirement years." Here you can try different figures for retirement income, return on savings, and inflation rate, and then watch the spreadsheet calculate the affect on your retirement cash flow. All of the calculations are based on your entries here and on entries made earlier. The table is built upon the formula we used to show the total of all savings. Cell B74, the Fund Total at age 65, simply displays the number in cell E4, the combined total of savings and annual contributions. Then, the spreadsheet displays the income we calculated would be needed for a comfortable retirement. The income figure is entered in cell C68 to make it easier for you to adjust the figures later; income is then copied to cell D74 to create the table that will project cash flow during the retirement years.

First you subtract income from the fund at age 65 to give you the balance of the fund at the end of the first year of retirement. Since the fund will continue to earn interest during that year, you want to add one year's interest. This won't be precise since money will be withdrawn at various times, but it's close enough.

This part of the spreadsheet uses a different interest rate than the earlier sections, because during retirement you'll probably invest your fund in more conservative instruments than you did before. The growth of the fund during retirement years is made using this interest rate. Inflation will continue to be a factor during retirement, so you also have built in an annual increase to the amount you plan to spend each

→ ## Where the money will go

The total amount saved based on our earlier projection

	A	B	C	D	E	F	G	H	I
60	94	$1,067,190		$1,705,448		$10,807,850		$13,580,487	
61	95	$1,173,909		$1,858,938		$11,996,714		$15,029,560	
62	96	$1,291,299		$2,026,242		$13,316,352		$16,633,894	
63									
64									
65	**Projecting cash flow in the retirement years**								
66									
67									
68		Income needed	$126,000						
69		Inflation rate	4%						
70		Interest on savings	0.05						
71									
72		Fund		Annual		Balance			
73		total		Spending		of Fund			
74	65	$1,418,736		$126,000		$1,292,736			
75	66	$1,357,372		$131,040		$1,226,332			
76	67	$1,226,332		$136,282		$1,090,051			
77	68	$1,090,051		$141,733		$948,318			
78	69	$948,318		$147,402		$800,916			
79	70	$800,916		$153,298		$647,617			
80	71	$647,617		$159,430		$488,187			
81	72	$488,187		$165,807		$322,380			
82	73	$322,380		$172,440		$149,940			
83	74	$149,940		$179,337		($29,397)			
84	75	($29,397)		$186,511		($215,908)			
85	76	($215,908)		$193,971		($409,879)			
86	77	($409,879)		$201,730		($611,609)			

The amount we calculated would be needed for a comfortable retirement in twenty years, adjusted for inflation.

Money is running out too soon.

year. The formula in column D under Annual Spending increases the amount of income by the inflation rate.

You won't have to study this table long to see that this retirement plan has a problem. At the current rate of savings, the comfortable retirement will last only until age 73. Sometime during the 74th year, the money will run out. Fortunately, our 45-year-old test case has time to fix the problem. Just about the only way to make the numbers work in this part of the spreadsheet is to lower the retirement income. Lowering the retirement income to $100,000 will buy an extra two years.

The formulas behind the retirement cash flow projection

Age is based on same range used earlier in the spreadsheet.

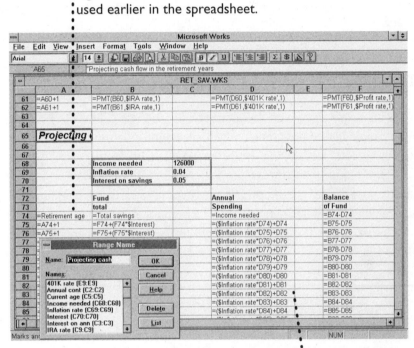

Annual spending is adjusted for inflation by multiplying last year's spending by the inflation rate in cell C69.

The better solution is to go up to the top and start increasing the value of the annual contribution. You can see both parts of the spreadsheet at one time by using the Split command on the Window menu. Most of us will find we need to increase the value in annual contribution until it starts to hurt—but it's better to feel the pain now while we're still young. You may also want to adjust some of the interest figures in the upper part of the spreadsheet if you have made conservative investments to reflect a move to aggressive investments. If your money is already invested aggressively, don't try to push your luck.

Regular use of a retirement planner like this spreadsheet can go a long way toward providing yourself with a comfortable retirement. But there is a dangerous side: Adjusting the numbers is easy. The hard part is taking on-screen projections and turning them into reality. Funding your retirement plan is a problem, and this spreadsheet can show you the solution. Remember that putting the money in solid investments is the real solution.

Getting the Most from Your Savings

Your first experience with these retirement planners is likely to be discouraging. Few people realize how much they'll need after inflation is factored into the equation.

Conservative investments like savings bonds and CDs can be counted on for steady growth, but they're probably not going to assure enough growth to provide a comfortable retirement. The salvation for most Americans lies in aggressive investing. The stock market has historically provided an average growth rate of 10 percent, but aggressive mutual funds may perform two or three percentage points higher. When you explore the effects of different interest rates in your retirement planners, you'll have a new appreciation for the value of improving your investments by even 1 percent a year.

Aggressive investing has risks but they're reduced over time. If you have more than 15 years to go before retirement age, you have plenty of time to let your investments ride through several market cycles, capturing the best and worst of the market. The trick is to have patience and not move your investments when the market is down. The market is prone to severe declines but it always comes back.

As retirement age grows closer, you'll want to move your investments out of growth stocks to avoid being caught in a down cycle when you need the money. Gradually move the money into conservative investments like money market funds and bonds. The age you do this depends on your personal philosophy. Conservative investors may want to move the entire fund out of aggressive investments as far as ten years ahead of retirement age. But they'll be denying themselves several years' worth of growth. In fact, many advisers are starting to recommend keeping a portion of your retirement fund in growth stocks even after retirement age as a defense against the ravages of inflation.

The key to managing your retirement account is to spread it out. Even during the times when the fund is mostly invested in aggressive investments, you'll want to use a variety of mutual funds or stocks. Later, as you move the money into conservative funds, move it gradually. For example, if you plan to move from aggressive to conservative investing ten years ahead of retirement age, you will have a goal of moving about 10 percent a year. But avoid moving it in large blocks. Sell the aggressive investments monthly or weekly to buy the conservative investments. For more help on investment philosophies and choosing specific investments, refer to Chapters 4, 5, and 6.

12

Estate *Planning*

192 Why You Need a Will

195 What You Can and Can't Do with WillMaker

199 Creating a Living Will

201 Organize Your Records for Posterity

```
 Print    Options   Zoom Out   <<
```

                    Will of Lois M

PERSONAL INFORMATION
I, Lois Mahler, a resident of Flo:
declare that this is my will. My :
is 123-45-6789.

REVOCATION OF PREVIOUS WILLS
FIRST. I revoke all wills and cod:

Almost
every day you face decisions about your finances. Many are pressing decisions and the choices have an immediate impact. But for too many people, the chore that ultimately has the greatest impact on their financial situation is ignored. People who fail to take a small amount of time to prepare a will place all of their hard-earned property at risk after they die. If you have any dependents, you risk impoverishing your loved ones if you don't leave a will.

Planning your estate does not require a great deal of time or expense. A simple-to-use computer program can guide you through the process, allowing you to do the entire job by yourself or to cut down on the expense of consulting a lawyer. In addition to preparing a will, a few other simple chores will help ensure that your assets go to the people you love and not to the state.

In this chapter, you'll decide if you need to consult a lawyer in preparing your will, learn how to prepare a will on your computer, and learn how to organize your records so your wishes will be carried out when you die.

Why You Need a Will

Wills are often perceived as having a glow of Hollywood mystique. We think of wills as devices to distribute the vast holdings of an estate where every knick-knack is worth thousands of dollars. When we think of our own property, we figure it will all go to our family anyway, so why waste money on paperwork for our humble possessions? The reason is that the laws in your state dictate how property not named in a will is distributed. You probably won't be happy with how the state plans to handle it.

What a Will Accomplishes

- ✔ Transfers ownership of property
- ✔ Names alternate beneficiaries in the event that a beneficiary dies
- ✔ Names a guardian for children under the age of 18
- ✔ Establishes how property left to minors will be managed
- ✔ Specifies how your debts and taxes will be paid
- ✔ Cancels debts owed to you
- ✔ Names an executor for your estate

States administer the property of the deceased through probate or surrogate courts. If a valid will is submitted to the court and it's not contested, the executor of an estate follows the will's directives in transferring property to each of the beneficiaries. When a valid will is found, the probate process extracts very little from the estate in terms of expenses or delays. If no will is found or a will is ruled to be invalid, the probate court will name an administrator to distribute the assets. This administrator, who will be paid a fee out of the estate, will follow the state's laws on how property is to be distributed, usually with the aid of an attorney who will also be paid from the estate. If you believe your estate is too small to merit the attention of a will, think of how much smaller it will be after it goes through probate!

Many people assume all of their modest possessions will be inherited by their spouse after they die. But in some states, if you have children, your spouse's share will be equal to the share of each child. Even if your spouse needs the money to raise the children, he or she could be blocked from using the children's share of the money. If the children are young, the state may prevent anyone from touching the money until the children are 18 when they'll be free to use the money any way they wish, even if they want to blow it all on a party.

Many married people assume their spouse will take care of the children after they're gone, but what if both parents die together? Without a will, the state appoints a guardian to make decisions about how and where the children are raised. The court-appointed guardian, who is paid a fee out of the estate, will decide how the children's property can be spent. Even if a close relative or family friend is willing to come forward and take on the responsibility of being guardian to the children, they'll need to spend money on a lawyer to guide them through the process of petitioning the court. And of course there's no guarantee they'll succeed in convincing the court to appoint them as guardians.

Even if you're unmarried and have no dependents, you probably won't be happy with what the state will do with your property. If you have no known relatives, the state will claim everything. If your parents are still alive, the courts will give it all to them (after the administrator is paid, of course). If you're unmarried and your parents are dead, the state will distribute the money to your nearest relatives, even if you never met them. A longtime roommate and companion may be successful in convincing the court they're entitled to a share of your estate, but the process will be costly.

➜ *Assets Not Covered by a Will*

One way to avoid disputes over how your property is distributed is to put everything into joint ownership. A will does not supersede the joint ownership of a bank account or a home, and it cannot change the beneficiary of an insurance policy. A will distributes only the property that is owned free and clear by the author of the will; if you named your brother as the beneficiary of your retirement account, that will not change because you name your son as beneficiary of the policy in your will.

The disadvantage of placing everything in joint ownership is that the arrangement is more permanent than a will. You can change a will as often as you wish, but to remove someone as joint owner of a home or bank account you need their consent. The beneficiary clause in a retirement account or insurance policy is more flexible, but it's common to forget about the people you've named in a beneficiary clause, running the risk of naming someone who's dead or forgetting to name a newborn child.

When you sit down to create your will, review the beneficiary clauses in all of your retirement accounts to make sure they're up to date. One common mistake is to set up a bank account as a joint account simply because you want to make it easy for a relative to help you manage the account. When you die, the person named as a co-owner of the account will become the sole owner of the account. If you want to give someone access to an account while retaining full ownership, name a power-of-attorney instead of creating a joint account.

You can spare your loved one from the unnecessary expense of court challenges and emotional heartache with a simple will. For about $50, you can buy WillMaker, an easy-to-use program that will guide you through the process of creating a will. You'll need less than an hour to set the record straight and ensure that your family and friends are protected. Of course, you may decide to spend many hours giving careful thought to how each of your possessions is dispersed; but you can avoid a very great deal of misery even if you put in just a little bit of time to create a will now.

What You Can and Can't Do with WillMaker

A number of will-writing programs are on the market today. I recommend Will-Maker because it is written by Nolo Press, which has devoted itself to publishing well-respected books and software designed to help the average person deal with legal matters.

WillMaker will guide you completely through the process of creating and printing a will.

WillMaker will guide you completely through the process of creating and printing a will. You'll receive instructions on how the will needs to be witnessed and on how to cut legal costs for your survivors later by adding a self-proving affidavit to your will. WillMaker is available for DOS, Windows, or the Mac. While the program is easy to use—it follows an interview process similar in style to tax programs—it also comes with a very detailed manual that explains the ramifications of your decisions, which can serve as a good education on the legal issues.

Writing your own will

WillMaker guides you through an interview. All you need to do is answer questions.

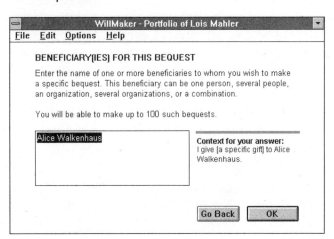

~ 🖥 ~

After you've used WillMaker to create a will, it's a good idea to have a lawyer review it, especially if you have a family lawyer who handles other business for you. Unless your lawyer is rigid in charging a set fee for preparing a will and is unwilling to accommodate you, you should find that you can cut your legal expenses by using WillMaker to create the will and then hiring a lawyer to review the document. Much of the expense in creating a will is the time your lawyer spends helping you decide how to allocate your property. If you can do that at home, reading through the manual and answering questions on your computer screen, you'll be ahead of the game. WillMaker claims its printed documents are valid in 49 of the 50 states—in Louisiana the Napoleonic code still rules, providing a different set of laws regarding estates and inheritance.

Because it's easy to start a new document or change an old one, plan to do a practice run first. You'll need a chance to become familiar with the language of naming beneficiaries, trustees, and guardians. (Be careful to destroy any versions of the will that are not final—the discovery of multiple versions of a will can wreak havoc on your estate.) After you've made your practice run, consult with your spouse or anyone else who you want to be involved in the process. Legally, you don't need to get the permission of someone you'll name as a guardian or executor, but you'll be on safer ground if you ask. A guardian will need to accept responsibilities he or she may not be prepared to accept. An executor's job can be very demanding and thankless, so you should choose someone who will be up to the task of negotiating with bankers and lawyers. The law does not provide for the direct compensation of a guardian or an executor so if you're naming friends or relatives you should take into account the expense you're asking them to shoulder.

Most people will find WillMaker able to prepare the paperwork for the will they want to create. If you have basic needs—naming a guardian for a dependent or giving your assets to specific individuals or organizations—WillMaker should be able to help you make the right decisions and to create the proper document. But if you have strong opinions about how your will should be prepared that go beyond a simple distribution of your properties, you'll need to hire a lawyer to prepare the will.

Making the will legal

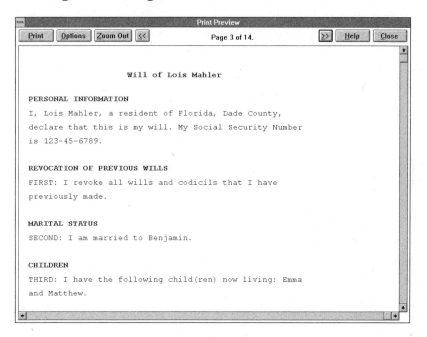

```
┌─────────────────────────────────────────────────────────────┐
│                        Print Preview                          │
│ [Print] [Options] [Zoom Out] [<<]    Page 3 of 14.   [>>] [Help] [Close] │
├─────────────────────────────────────────────────────────────┤
│                                                               │
│                     Will of Lois Mahler                       │
│                                                               │
│   PERSONAL INFORMATION                                        │
│   I, Lois Mahler, a resident of Florida, Dade County,         │
│   declare that this is my will. My Social Security Number     │
│   is 123-45-6789.                                             │
│                                                               │
│   REVOCATION OF PREVIOUS WILLS                                │
│   FIRST: I revoke all wills and codicils that I have          │
│   previously made.                                            │
│                                                               │
│   MARITAL STATUS                                              │
│   SECOND: I am married to Benjamin.                           │
│                                                               │
│   CHILDREN                                                    │
│   THIRD: I have the following child(ren) now living: Emma     │
│   and Matthew.                                                │
│                                                               │
└─────────────────────────────────────────────────────────────┘
```

After you answer WillMaker's questions, the program generates a carefully worded document that will become a will if it's properly signed and witnessed.

The attorneys who wrote WillMaker's legal language take a very conservative stance. Their primary goal is to make sure any will you create with the software stands up in court. As a result, the software is somewhat limiting. It prevents you from structuring your will in ways that are perfectly legal but which require very precise language. If you're considering one of the following strategies, you'll need to consult a lawyer. You may still want to try WillMaker for help in making decisions on other aspects of your estate so you'll cut down on the length of time you need to consult with your lawyer.

If you are in one of these situations, you'll need an attorney to draw up your will.

➡ You have a large estate and you could avoid inheritance taxes by setting up a trust. Contrary to popular opinion, trusts are not the exclusive reserve of the wealthy. Anyone with over $600,000 in property may benefit from distributing assets with a trust rather than a will since federal inheritance taxes start at that threshhold. The process of setting up a trust is not a major legal challenge, but it will require that you use a lawyer.

➡ You'd like the reading of your will to include an explanation of why you're bequeathing property to a certain person. WillMaker will guide you through the process of drafting a separate letter that you can store with your will to be read separately. This addendum serves the same legal purpose as including the information in the will itself, but of course it will not generate the same cinematic atmosphere at the reading of the will. You'll have to hire a lawyer if you've got your heart set on such a dramatic reading.

➡ You and your spouse want to create a joint will. In the past, joint wills were common, but they have led to so many complications that Will-Maker will not let you create one. Among the problems are the difficulty a surviving spouse faces in changing any terms of the will. And if any property is in the name of only one, the state may claim ownership. A joint will is so fraught with possible problems that it's best to have a lawyer draft the papers.

➡ You want to bequeath property only under certain conditions. (This scenario is, too, played out in many films: The wayward son will inherit the family fortune only if he gets a haircut, gives up his friends, and starts working in the family business.) You can structure your will with conditions if you wish, but you'll also need to set up a mechanism for monitoring the situation, and a lawyer will need to write it up.

➡ You want to name more than one guardian for a child. A joint guardianship is rarely a good idea even if the two guardians are married. The law will let you name joint guardians but in order to create an elaborate enough contingency plan in the event the joint guardianship does not work out, you'll need a lawyer to help you consider your options.

One of the benefits of using a lawyer is the discipline he or she brings to the process. A lawyer will make sure you have the right number of witnesses, the signatures are in the right places, and the will is safely stored. If you use WillMaker, you must be extremely careful to follow precisely both the instructions the program prints with your will and the directions in Chapter 9 of the manual, "Making It Legal: Final Steps." If the will is not signed and witnessed properly, the document may be ruled invalid. While the instructions the program prints with your will give you a general guideline, other directions are found only in the manual. For example, the witnesses who sign your will cannot be named in the will as beneficiaries; this bit of advice is found only in the manual.

If your affairs are relatively uncomplicated and you believe your instructions will be agreed to by all of your heirs, small mistakes in the will's preparation may not be a problem (a probate court judge will have the final word). But if you believe your will is likely to be contested, be sure to have a lawyer review the document since any minor error in executing the document can open the door to a long court battle.

Creating a Living Will

Creating a will helps your heirs by simplifying their process of carrying on after you're gone. But we all need to be concerned with how our families will deal with the possibility that we will require extended medical care. Making sure you're covered by medical insurance is only one part of the responsibility. It's also become important to let your family know how you would prefer to be treated in a hospital if you were unable to express your wishes. WillMaker can help in this area, too.

WillMaker guides you through the process of creating a living will, a document that clearly states your preference in choosing healthcare in the event that doctors want to employ extreme measures to keep you alive when you're unable to respond. A living will not only helps you to receive only the treatment you would choose but also it spares your immediate family from having to make agonizing decisions. For example, the program asks you to specify whether or not

Make your healthcare choices binding by creating a living will.

WillMaker can help you prepare a living will to guide your family through a difficult ordeal.

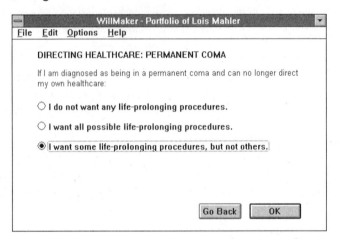

you would choose to be placed on a respirator if you're diagnosed with a terminal condition. WillMaker leads you through a series of medical situations, allowing you to choose among specific treatments. When you're done, the program prints a document that can be used by your friends and family in discussions with doctors.

A living will does not spare your family from all of the pain of consulting with doctors if you're faced with a terminal illness, but it will ease some of the burden. Hospital administrators and doctors who are reluctant to deny life-sustaining procedures are far more likely to defer to a relative's insistence that extraordinary efforts not be taken if they see a patient's wishes expressed in writing. And if your preference is that every possible medical procedure be explored in a situation the doctors diagnose as terminal, you'll save your family from having to agonize over their decisions.

Living wills are not on completely solid legal footing. Some states provide legal obstacles to patients whose directives contradict medical authorities. But the U.S. Supreme Court has upheld the concept of a living will as long as the patient's wishes are clear and explicit. WillMaker creates a document designed to satisfy that requirement. If you choose to use this part of the program, read the document very carefully before you sign it to make sure it does express your wishes.

Organize Your Records for Posterity

All of your careful planning will do little good if your will is never found. Franklin Roosevelt made very elaborate plans for his own funeral, but even though he was President of the United States when he died, his plans were never carried out because they weren't found until after the funeral. You don't need to post your will on your refrigerator door, but you should make an effort to organize your records so the will is discovered. Many married couples make the mistake of assuming the spouse knows everything; but even if you tell your spouse where everything is hidden and your spouse survives you, there's no guarantee he or she will be in the proper frame of mind to deal with a will at the necessary time.

Your family will be better protected if you take one of two approaches. Either organize your files in such a clear fashion that it will be obvious to any friend of the family where everything can be found; or create a simple document explaining where the most important papers, such as your will, are stored.

For the first approach to work, first make certain your family's financial records are within plain sight. If everything's stored in a remote corner of the attic, it may be months before the papers are discovered. Or if you have an extensive system of files in a commonly used area of your home, make sure your personal papers are labeled so someone else will be able to find the will and key financial records.

The second approach may make sense even if you have organized your records well. One of the problems an executor will face is to locate records identifying all of the accounts covered by the will, including statements from banks, mutual fund companies, stock brokers, and insurance companies. WillMaker helps by providing a thick parchment envelope that clearly labels the document inside as a will.

When you finalize a will, take great care to ensure that this is the only version of the will in print. The discovery of an earlier will can invalidate your final will and necessitate a court ruling. Before you complete a will, make sure you have destroyed any earlier versions. A good strategy is to keep a copy of your will in your records and a copy in the records of either your attorney, a close friend, or a relative.

In some states, the worst place to store a will is a safe deposit box. The law in some states requires banks to seal the safe deposit boxes when the owner dies. Some states allow executors to have free access to a safe deposit box, but if the will naming your executor is locked inside the box, you will have needlessly complicated delayed things for your survivors. If you store your will in a safe deposit box, make sure your executor knows where it is and is given access to the box on your bank's records.

As you're filing your will, take a few minutes to make sure the rest of your records are in good shape. Will your survivors be able to find records of your bank accounts, mutual funds, and insurance policies? A good practice is to write up a short list of major assets, listing the names of your accounts, your social security number, the name of insurance agents, and the location of a safe deposit box. Write up a list using a word processor. Every year or so, you should revise the list, adding new investments and deleting old ones. By using a word processor, you'll have to do the bulk of the work just once; keeping it up to date will be an easy chore.

If you track your investments in Quicken, the chore can be made very simple. You can create a summary of your investments by using Quicken to generate a report showing all your investments and bank accounts, and then export it into a word processor. While you may be satisfied with the report printed directly from Quicken, you'll have better records if you customize the report in a word processor. That way, you can add account balances, names of the owners (including joint ownership if necessary), and any other information your feel your executor may need, such as the name of a broker who manages the account.

To create this type of report, open Quicken and select Other and then Account Balances from the Reports menu. Quicken will show a summary of all

Summarizing your accounts with Quicken

Create a summary report of all your accounts and keep it with your will.

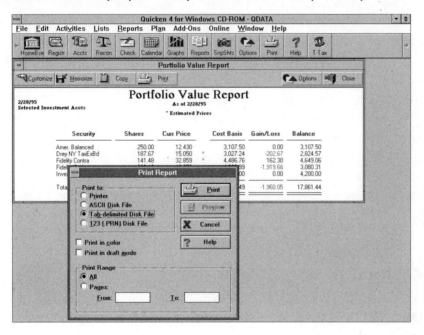

your accounts, with the current balances. Make sure all of your accounts are displayed. If you used this option in the past, you may have customized the display so that some accounts are excluded; you can fix it by using the Customize button. Once you've tailored the display to show all of your investments, select the Print button and then select the option to print to a tab-delimited disk file. Then you'll be prompted for a name and a directory. The file that Quicken saves will be a text file any word processor can read. Quit Quicken, run your favorite word processor, and open this file. You'll need to play with options for tabs and margins in order to get a good display of your accounts. But once you have the data displayed properly, you can add any notes you feel your executor will need. Print the file from your word processor and keep it in the same file as your will.

Appendix A: *Guide to the CD-ROM*

The CD-ROM accompanying this book comes with an installation program that will copy the programs and files on the disk to your hard disk. Or, you can copy the individual files directly to your hard disk using a file manager. Every spreadsheet file is available in three formats: WKS files are in Microsoft Works format; WK1 files in Lotus 1-2-3 format and XLS files are for Microsoft Excel. The TXT files can be read by any word processor.

The disk contains a copy of WinCIM, a program that will connect with you CompuServe and provide you with several free hours of connect time. The disk also includes includes spreadsheets, help files, and programs discussed at length in the book. The files discussed in the book can be found in directories that match the chapters in the book. For example, files mentioned in Chapter 2 are in the directory \CHAPTER.2. You'll find detailed discussion of most of these programs in the appropriate chapter. Following is a summary of each of the files.

Chapter 2

ALIGN.TXT   Help in fixing Quicken check-printing problems.
QIF.TXT   A detailed explanation of the Quicken Interchange Format (QIF) that will be essential if you plan to import Quicken QIF files into any other application.

Chapter 3

CHECKBK   A spreadsheet checkbook manager. Simply begin to enter the same information you would enter into a paper checkbook register and the spreadsheet will keep a running balance.
CR_CDSAV   A spreadsheet that will calculate the amount you earn on the float of a credit card if you pay off the balance in full each month.

Chapter 6

EEBOND   A program that will track your savings bonds, showing you the current value of each and the date when the bond stops paying interest. This is a shareware program; if you use the program you should register it with the author and pay the author's fee. Since the government updates the return on savings bonds periodically, you will need to register the program and obtain future releases. One free update will be sent to you when you register the program.

Chapter 7

INV_CAT A spreadsheet you can use to create an inventory of your household contents to help you prepare insurance claims.
TERM_WHO A spreadsheet that compares premiums on a term life insurance policy versus a whole life policy.
T_W_CASH A spreadsheet you can use to compare the cost of a whole life insurance policy with a term policy, including the cash value.

Chapter 8

MORTGAGE A spreadsheet that will track all of the costs in a home purchase, including closing costs. Use the spreadsheet to determine the amount of cash you'll need to buy a house and the monthly payment.
CARBUY A spreadsheet that you can use to compare the cost of buying a car versus leasing. It will track options, as well as miscellaneous costs, like registration fees.
ARM A shareware program for calculating the savings in an adjustable rate mortgage, compared to a fixed rate mortgage. The program shows how much either method will cost you, projected out for the life of the loan. This program is shareware; if you like the program and continue to use it, you should register it and pay the author's fee.
POINTS A program for comparing the cost of buying points on a mortgage against the cost of a mortgage with no points. The program shows how much you will pay each month by either method over the full life of the mortgage. This program is shareware; if you like the program and continue to use it, you should register it and pay the author's fee.

Chapter 9

COLLEGE1, COLLEGE2, COLLEGE3, and **COLLEGE4** Spreadsheets that will help parents project the cost of tuition for their children and estimate how much they need to save each year. There are four versions of the spreadsheet,

COLLEGE1 is for parents of one child, COLLEGE2 is for parents of two children, and so on.

Chapter 11

RET_NEED   A spreadsheet to help you estimate the amount of annual income you'll need at retirement age.

RET_SAVE   A spreadsheet designed to help you track the value of your retirement savings and determine how much you need to add to your retirement savings in order to reach your retirement income goal.

Appendix B: Where to Find It

CompuServe	800–848–8199
IRS help line	800–829–1040
MECA Software	800–288–6322
Microsoft Works	800–434–3978
Nolo Press	510–549–1976
ProComm	314–443–4383
Prodigy	800–PRODIGY
Quicken	800–624–8742
Social Security Administration	800–772–1213
TurboTax	800–964–1040

Index

accounts, setting up,
19–23

account statements, 4,
24–25

aggressive investments,
188–189

America Online mutual
fund service, 65–66

ARM program (on
provided CD-
ROM), 141

assets not covered by a
will, 194

ATM withdrawals,
tracking with
Quicken, 45

AutoNet, 52, 131–132

average American
spending, 39

backing up your work,
14–15

backup disks, making,
14–15

bank statements, 4, 24–25

bill paying. *See* paying
bills

bond funds. *See* mutual
funds

bonds
corporate, 57
government savings,
57, 98–102
vs. stocks, 58

brokers
discount vs. full-
service, 76–77
online, 90–93

budgeting
household, 17–35
need for, 38
with Quicken, 40–42

buying, online, 50, 52–53

buying a car, 50, 52,
127–135
calculating payments,
133–135
finding dealer cost,
131–132
loan or lease, 127–135

buying a house, 135–142

Calendar (Quicken), 29

canceled checks, keeping,
172

capital appreciation of
investments, 64

car, financing. *See* buying
a car

CARBUY.WK1
spreadsheet (on
provided CD-
ROM), 129

cash, tracking with
Quicken, 44–46

categories (Microsoft
Works), 33

categories (Quicken)
changing, 164
sub- and super-
categories, 44
using, 41–44

Categories & Transfers
(Quicken), 165–166

CD-ROM (with this book)
ARM program, 141
CARBUY.WK1
spreadsheet, 129
COLLEGE1.WKS and
COLLEGE2.WKS,
149
EEBOND program, 101
MORTGAGE.WK1
spreadsheet,
136–142
POINTS program, 142
RET_NEEDS.WKS
spreadsheet,
177–181

RET_SAV.WKS
spreadsheet, 181
CDs (certificates of
deposit), 98
checkbook, methods of
keeping, 19–23
CheckFree bill-paying
service, 34–35
checking account
statements, 4
check printing, 22–23.
See also paying bills
check register, 19, 24,
30–33
closed-end mutual funds,
57
Clothing expense
category, 43
clutter, clearing, 2–5
college costs
funding strategies,
149–153
getting information on,
146–149
paying for, 145–156
rise in, 146
savings plan for,
154–156
COLLEGE1.WKS and
COLLEGE2.WKS
(on provided CD-
ROM), 149
Company Analyzer (on
CompuServe), 83

CompuServe, 10
AutoNet on, 132
charting stock history
on, 83
Company Analyzer on,
83
FundWatch on, 66–69
money-market
shopping on, 97–98
Money menu on, 81
navigating in, 84
Peterson's College
Database on, 148
stock research on,
80–85
TurboTax on, 170
CompuServe Information
Manager (CIM), 84
CompuServe Navigator
(CSNav), 84
conservative investments,
188–189
Consumer Reports, 50
copying files, 30
credit cards
proper use of, 46–50
tracking charges, 25,
51
current balance
calculation formula,
32
cutting spending, 37–53

data files
copying, 30
managing, 2–3, 30
deed, house, 4
Dining expense category,
39, 43
discount brokers, 76–77
discretionary expenses,
assessing, 38
disk in this book. *See* CD-
ROM (with this
book)
dollar cost averaging, 61
Dow Jones, researching
stocks with, 78–80

Edgar (information server
for the Internet), 89
Enter key, using in
Quicken, 27
Entertainment expense
category, 43
envelopes (window),
23–25
estate planning, 191–203
Excel spreadsheet
formulas, 133–135
expense categories, 33,
38–39, 43

expenses, necessary vs. discretionary, 38

files
  copying, 30
  managing, 2–3, 30
Fill Series command, 151–152
Financial Calendar (Quicken), 29
financial management tools, selecting, 7–11
formulas. *See* spreadsheet formulas
full-service brokers, 76–77
FundWatch (on CompuServe), 66–69
future of personal financial management, 33–35
FV (future value) formula, 155–156, 183–184

getting organized, 1–15
government savings bonds, 57, 98–102

home inventory, creating, 116–122
Hoover Company Database (on CompuServe), 81–82
house buying, 135–142
household budget, assembling, 17–35

information highway, 12
Innovest Technical Analysis (Dow Jones), 79–80
insurance, homeowners, 116–122
insurance, life. *See* life insurance
Intellicharge service (Quicken), 51
interest on savings, shopping for rates, 96–98
Internet
  connecting to, 90
  researching stocks, 88–90
inventory (home), creating, 116–122

InvesText (on CompuServe), 83–85
investing. *See* mutual funds; stocks
investments, aggressive vs. conservative, 188–189
IRS, getting help from, 170
IRS audits, 5
  and keeping good records, 172
  TurboTax anticipates, 171

leasing a car, 127–135
life insurance, 105–116
  assessing your needs, 106–110
  cashing in the policy, 116
  shopping for a policy, 110–116
  types of, 112–113
living will, creating, 199–201
loan calculator (Quicken), 128
loans, 125–135

Managing Your Money
package, 9, 108–110

Market Monitor (Dow
Jones), 78–80

married people, need for
a will, 193

memorized transactions
(Quicken), 164

Microsoft Excel
spreadsheet
formulas, 133–135

Microsoft Money, 9

Microsoft Works (*see also*
spreadsheets)

categorizing expenses,
33

creating a range name,
150–151

downloading fund
information to,
65–66

Fill Series command,
151–152

spreadsheet formula
structure, 133–135

spreadsheets, 11

mini-register, 48–49

modem, 12–14

money-market account
rates, 96–98

Money Watch (on
CompuServe), 67

mortgages, 135–142

paying points, 141–142

shopping for, 138–142

tax deductibility of,
167–168

types of, 141

MORTGAGE.WK1 (on
provided CD-
ROM), 136–142

mutual funds, 55–73

choosing a strategy,
61–63

finding by ticker
symbols, 63–64

forms of payment, 61

fund company charges,
62

need to invest in, 56

online shopping for,
63–69

principle of, 56

risk classifications,
61–63

sampler, 58

terms used with, 60

tracking, 70–73

ways they are sold, 57

old statements, entering
data from, 24–25

online brokers, 90–93

online services, 34

buying mutual funds,
63–69

features of, 52

saving reports from, 79

stock investing with,
76–93

using, 10–11

online shopping, 50,
52–53

open-end mutual funds,
57

paperwork. *See*
recordkeeping

parallel port, 13

paying bills

by Calendar using
Quicken, 29

using CheckFree,
34–35

with window
envelopes, 23–25

PC Financial Network (on
Prodigy), 93

personal financing
management

basic toolkit, 8

future of, 33–35

Peterson's College
Database, 148

PMT (payment) formula,
133–135

points, in mortgage financing, 141–142

POINTS program (on provided CD-ROM), 142

policies, saving, 4

printers, 22–23

printing checks, 22–23

ProComm, 13–14

Prodigy, 10, 34

  mutual fund service, 65–66

  placing a stock buy order, 93

  stock research on, 80, 85–88

proofs of purchase, 5–6, 172

QDATA (Quicken data) files, managing, 30

QIF_HELP.TXT, 30

QIF (Quicken Interchange Format) files, 30–31

Quicken. *See also* transactions (Quicken)

  budgeting with, 40–42

  calculations in, 10

  categorizing spending with, 41–44

changing categories in, 164

choosing the right version of, 20

Financial Calendar in, 29

fine-tuning accounts in, 28–30

Home Inventory in, 117, 119

Intellicharge service of, 51

introduction to, 8–9

loan calculator in, 128

looking up a name from a list in, 9

managing data files in, 30

navigating with the Tab key, 25–27

quick entry tips, 28

QuickFill feature, 27

Reconciliation feature, 27

Setup program, 19, 21

summarizing accounts in, 202–203

super- and subcategories in, 44

Tax Planner, 161–163

toolbar, 21

tracking cash with, 44–46

tracking mutual funds with, 70–71

tracking tax expenses with, 164–168

using Categories & Transfers, 165–166

using with TurboTax, 167

Write Checks screen, 26

QuoteCom database, 90

range names, using in spreadsheets, 150–152

receipts, keeping, 5–6, 172

Reconciliation feature of Quicken, 27

recordkeeping

  organizing papers, 1–15

  for posterity, 201–203

  reasons for, 5

  and taxes, 172

  throwing away papers, 3–5

  what is worth keeping, 7

register, checkbook, 19, 24, 30–33

retirement planning,
175–189
getting the most from
savings, 188–189
how long savings will
last, 185–188
the income you will
need, 176–181
projecting growth of
savings, 181–185
time as best ally, 176
RET_NEEDS.WKS (on
provided CD-
ROM), 177–181
RET_SAV.WKS (on
provided CD-
ROM), 181

safe-deposit box, 4
savings, 95–102
finding the best
interest rates,
96–98, 188–189
how long they will
last, 185–188
planning for college
costs, 154–156
projecting growth of,
181–185
recommended rate of,
38

savings account
statements, 4
savings bonds, 57–58,
98–102
scheduled transactions in
Quicken, 28–29
security of backup disks,
14–15
serial port, 13
Series EE savings bonds,
99
Setup program for
Quicken, 19, 21
shares. *See* stocks
shopping online, 50,
52–53
Social Security, 179–181
Social Security survivor's
benefits, 108
spending
average American, 39
cutting, 37–53
splitting transactions, 46,
48–49
spreadsheet formulas
behind home-buyer's
worksheet, 140
behind monthly
savings calculation,
156
behind retirement cash
flow projection, 187

behind retirement
income projections,
180
behind retirement
savings plan, 184
behind tuition
projection, 153
FV (future value),
155–156, 183–184
PMT (payment),
133–135
structure of, 133–135
VLOOKUP, 179–180,
183–184
spreadsheet ranges, using,
150–152
spreadsheets, 7 (*see also*
Microsoft Works)
advantages and
disadvantages of, 31
building a check
register, 30–33
for home inventory,
119–122
for life insurance
assessments, 107
for life insurance cost
comparison,
114–115
for mutual fund
tracking, 71–73
stock brokers
charges, 62

discount vs. full-
service, 76–77
online, 90–93
stocks
downloading and
saving reports, 79
finding investment
tips, 85, 89
investing in, 75–93
investing on your own,
77–78, 90
researching with
CompuServe, 80–85
researching with Dow
Jones, 78–80
researching on the
Internet, 88–90
researching with
Prodigy, 80, 85–88
vs. return on bonds, 58
risks of, 60
simulating trading of,
91
Strategic Investor (on
Prodigy), 87
subcategories in Quicken,
44
summarizing your
accounts with
Quicken, 202–203
super-categories in
Quicken, 44

Tab key in Quicken,
25–27
TaxCut tax preparation
program, 31
taxes, 159–173 (*see also*
TurboTax)
deductibility of
mortgage payments,
167–168
filing an electronic
return, 173
getting help from the
IRS, 170
head-start versions of
tax software, 166
and IRS audits, 5,
171–172
tax-related transactions
in Quicken, 165
tracking deductible
expenses, 45,
164–168
Tax Planner (Quicken),
161–163
term life insurance, 112
throwing papers away, 3–5
ticker symbols, using to
find a fund, 63–64
toolkit for personal
finances, 8

tools (financial
management),
selecting, 7–11
Tradeline service (on
Prodigy), 86–87
transactions (Quicken)
common tax-related,
165
dragging to a date, 29
recording, 24–27
scheduled, 28–29
splitting, 46
types of, 6–7
TurboTax, 160–161, 163
(*see also* taxes)
getting help from,
169–171
using the Interview,
168–171
using with Quicken
categories, 167
using the reality check
feature, 169–170

universal life insurance,
112
unmarried people, need
for a will, 193
U.S. savings bonds, 57,
98–102

variable life insurance,
113
version of Quicken,
choosing, 20
VLOOKUP formula,
179–180, 183–184

ZD Press Books Plus, 12
ZiffNet, 12

Wall St. Edge (on
Prodigy), 88
W–4 Estimator
(TurboTax), 163
whole life insurance, 113
WillMaker program,
194–197, 199–201
creating a living will,
199–201
writing your will with,
195–197
wills
assets not covered by,
194
giving heirs access to,
201–202
need for, 192–194
and summarizing your
assets, 202–203
writing, 195–197
window envelopes, 23–25
Write Checks screen
(Quicken), 26

Ziff-Davis Press Survey of Readers

Please help us in our effort to produce the best books on personal computing.
For your assistance, we would be pleased to send you a FREE catalog
featuring the complete line of Ziff-Davis Press books.

1. How did you first learn about this book?

Recommended by a friend . . . . ☐ -1 (5)
Recommended by store personnel . . . . ☐ -2
Saw in Ziff-Davis Press catalog . . . . ☐ -3
Received advertisement in the mail . . . . ☐ -4
Saw the book on bookshelf at store . . . . ☐ -5
Read book review in: _____ ☐ -6
Saw an advertisement in: _____ ☐ -7
Other (Please specify): _____ ☐ -8

2. Which THREE of the following factors most influenced your decision to purchase this book? (Please check up to THREE.)

Front or back cover information on book . . .☐ -1 (6)
Logo of magazine affiliated with book . . . . . .☐ -2
Special approach to the content . . . .☐ -3
Completeness of content . . . .☐ -4
Author's reputation. . . . .☐ -5
Publisher's reputation . . . .☐ -6
Book cover design or layout . . . .☐ -7
Index or table of contents of book . . . .☐ -8
Price of book . . . .☐ -9
Special effects, graphics, illustrations . . . . . .☐ -0
Other (Please specify): _____ ☐ -x

3. How many computer books have you purchased in the last six months? _____ (7-10)

4. On a scale of 1 to 5, where 5 is excellent, 4 is above average, 3 is average, 2 is below average, and 1 is poor, please rate each of the following aspects of this book below. (Please circle your answer.)

Depth/completeness of coverage	5	4	3	2	1	(11)
Organization of material	5	4	3	2	1	(12)
Ease of finding topic	5	4	3	2	1	(13)
Special features/time saving tips	5	4	3	2	1	(14)
Appropriate level of writing	5	4	3	2	1	(15)
Usefulness of table of contents	5	4	3	2	1	(16)
Usefulness of index	5	4	3	2	1	(17)
Usefulness of accompanying disk	5	4	3	2	1	(18)
Usefulness of illustrations/graphics	5	4	3	2	1	(19)
Cover design and attractiveness	5	4	3	2	1	(20)
Overall design and layout of book	5	4	3	2	1	(21)
Overall satisfaction with book	5	4	3	2	1	(22)

5. Which of the following computer publications do you read regularly; that is, 3 out of 4 issues?

Byte . . . . ☐ -1 (23)
Computer Shopper . . . . ☐ -2
Home Office Computing . . . . ☐ -3
Dr. Dobb's Journal . . . . ☐ -4
LAN Magazine . . . . ☐ -5
MacWEEK . . . . ☐ -6
MacUser . . . . ☐ -7
PC Computing . . . . ☐ -8
PC Magazine . . . . ☐ -9
PC WEEK . . . . ☐ -0
Windows Sources . . . . ☐ -x
Other (Please specify): _____ ☐ -y

Please turn page.

6. What is your level of experience with personal
computers? With the subject of this book?

	With PCs	With subject of book
Beginner............	☐ -1 (24)	☐ -1 (25)
Intermediate..........	☐ -2	☐ -2
Advanced.............	☐ -3	☐ -3

7. Which of the following best describes your job title?

Officer (CEO/President/VP/owner)........ ☐ -1 (26)
Director/head......................... ☐ -2
Manager/supervisor.................... ☐ -3
Administration/staff.................. ☐ -4
Teacher/educator/trainer.............. ☐ -5
Lawyer/doctor/medical professional....... ☐ -6
Engineer/technician.................... ☐ -7
Consultant.......................... ☐ -8
Not employed/student/retired............ ☐ -9
Other (Please specify): _____ ☐ -0

8. What is your age?

Under 20........................... ☐ -1 (27)
21-29............................ ☐ -2
30-39............................ ☐ -3
40-49............................ ☐ -4
50-59............................ ☐ -5
60 or over......................... ☐ -6

9. Are you:

Male............................. ☐ -1 (28)
Female............................ ☐ -2

Thank you for your assistance with this important
information! Please write your address below to
receive our free catalog.

Name: _____

Address: _____

City/State/Zip: _____

Fold here to mail.   3016-16-19

_____

_____

_____

BUSINESS REPLY MAIL
FIRST CLASS MAIL   PERMIT NO. 1612   OAKLAND, CA

POSTAGE WILL BE PAID BY ADDRESSEE

Ziff-Davis Press
ZD PRESS 5903 Christie Avenue
Emeryville, CA 94608-1925
Attn: Marketing

NO POSTAGE
NECESSARY
IF MAILED IN
THE UNITED
STATES